Do unto others
as though
you were
the
others

—Elbert Hubbard

A THOUSAND &
ONE EPIGRAMS

and

THE ROYCROFT SHOP:
A HISTORY

by

ELBERT HUBBARD

A THOUSAND &
ONE EPIGRAMS

and

THE ROYCROFT SHOP:
A HISTORY

by

ELBERT HUBBARD

Edited for Today by
NANCY HUBBARD BRADY

PRENTICE-HALL

Englewood Cliffs   New Jersey

CONTENTS

PREFACE

*E*LBERT HUBBARD *met a tragic death in the sinking of the S. S. Lusitania by a German U-boat on May 7, 1915. He was more famous in his day, and probably is best remembered today, for his classic motivational essay,* A Message to Garcia, *now well past 80 million copies in reprints. Another of his works,* A Thousand & One Epigrams, *long overshadowed by the "Message" is at long last emerging as a link between the generations since Hubbard's heyday.*

Aside from having been a prolific ad man, writer, public and employee relations pioneer, and magazine editor-publisher, Hubbard was among the highest paid lecturers on the Orpheum Circuit at the turn of the century. In all of these communications fields he knew well the importance of getting across a point with as few words as possible. His longest discourses, verbal or written, really were made up of well-connected series of epigrams.

Today, nearly sixty years after his death,

PREFACE

Hubbard's most popular epigrams are to be seen in magazines and newspapers or heard quoted by public speakers with amazing regularity. This pandemic appeal is all the more remarkable when one realizes his first edition of "1001 EPIGRAMS" has been out of print for over half a century.

Joe Mitchell Chapple, biographical writer, speaker, movie producer, and one-time editor of National Magazine (Boston), tells in his Foreword to Mary Hubbard Heath's The Elbert Hubbard I Knew *of bantering with Hubbard on the subject of the probable lasting value of the latter's works.*

Hubbard reportedly drew a book of bound manuscripts from his library shelf and handing it to Chapple, said, "Here is some of my stuff that may live long after my chair is vacant. It's great fun to imagine comments of future generations on what you admit are immortal thoughts on paper!"

Hubbard would be elated to know there is more and more comment, pro and con, about his "immortal thoughts" these days. But it is the growing current enthusiasm and adoption of his sayings by persons of the new right, center and left that seems now to assure him of a lasting place among American writers and philosophers—something that neither Chapple nor Hubbard could have really, deep-down anticipated.

With love as his watchword, wisdom his guide, and brevity his style, Hubbard's purpose in expression was always one and universal—that the substance by which we mold our lives be Truth. As exemplified by his own life, this was his earnest appeal to all mankind.

A high school dropout, he truly worked his way up to the top in the business world. Then, more bored than disillusioned, he chucked it for the world of arts and letters. But, knowing by experience that it wasn't all bad or, indeed, bad at all for those who liked that mode of life, he used the good he had learned from it to help him pursue the life he preferred. He didn't refuse to board the merry-go-round; he got on, took a good ride to see all sides, and then got off. Indeed Elbert Hubbard was something of a humanist and much of his philosophy was hand, head and heart tested. The thoughts

PREFACE

poured forth from his own crucible of experience, fired by the same searching flame that strangely bonds peace with unrest, and success with failure today.

When he said, somewhat cryptically, "Fences are only for those who cannot fly," he may have confused many of his turn-of-the century followers who were perhaps better attuned to his more direct, Franklinesque sayings. But, like the "Dare dream!" exhortation itself, that epigram of his has remained aloft to drift down, 70 years later, long enough to be reflected upon by visionaries today.

The eldest of the three of us who have co-authored this preface was but six months old when her grandfather died. The other two, his great-granddaughter Linda, and her husband Ted, had numerous discussions with their friends on the relevancy of Elbert Hubbard today. Among their conclusions were:

Elbert Hubbard wrote so much about Friendship, Life, Love, Men, Women and Work—our topics for discussion today; he wasn't a fence-straddler; he kept it simple,

PREFACE

evidently through his own strength; he didn't stumble over simplicity like we sometimes do—he could perceive the obvious; he didn't sit in judgment of his fellow men; Hubbard must have really 'lived'— he wrote on so many subjects: Hubbard talked 'quality' not 'quantity';, this book has something for everyone—for the curious, the heart that is hungry, the seeker of truth and reality, all the way up to the intellectual.

Elbert Hubbard was not concerned with fashions or modes of attire; he simply dressed for the occasion. But his long hair and soft, black, flowing tie were trademarks of the man. His appearance being what it was, during a lecture it wasn't unusual to hear cries of castigation from disapproving members of his audience. Hubbard later wrote, "I would miss the ripe ribaldry to which, for a score of years, mine ears have become accustomed. Like men who have worked in boiler shops; I crave the chorus of the merry hammer."

We have been raised on Elbert Hubbard's epigrammatic philosophy, treasured and handed down to us by his son, Elbert Hub-

PREFACE

bard II, a great man in his own right who was nonetheless great for never having claimed to be smarter than his father.

This edition of A Thousand & One Epigrams is edited for today's readers by Elbert Hubbard's descendants with a light touch of the editorial pencil; no heavier attention seemed to be needed. A few repetitious or totally obscure passages have been omitted, nevertheless allowing 1281 epigrams to remain—a generous margin over the "1001" promised in the title. A few notes have been added to explain terms not readily found in a modern reader's dictionary. (On page 71 the name "Padmarx" appears. Our most diligent research failed to come up with a note of explanation, but we liked the epigram and let it stand in our edition. The "House of Hubbard" would be happy to hear from any reader who may cast some light on the meaning of "Padmarx.") And, we have expanded the Index so that it may be used more readily than for the original edition, to locate a favorite epigram, or to explore a theme.

Aside from these changes, the publisher has provided a faithful facsimile copy of the

PREFACE

original which bore this characteristic colophon:

SO HERE THEN ENDETH THIS
MOST WORTHY BOOK, *ONE THOU-
SAND AND ONE EPIGRAMS*, THE
SAME BEING ORPHIC SAYINGS
EVOLVED IN IDLE MOMENTS BY
ELBERT HUBBARD, AND GATH-
ERED TOGETHER AND DONE INTO
A PRINTED VOLUME BY THE ROY-
CROFTERS AT THEIR SHOP, AT EAST
AURORA, IN THE YEAR MCMXI.

*Elbert Hubbard's ideas, when not time-
less, were, at the very least, far ahead of his
time. Particularly indicative of his almost
mystical influence and rapport with the generations that were to follow him on this
basically good old earth that he dearly loved,
is the* Roycroft *concept. To give the reader
a revealing view of the foundation and the
flourishing of the* Roycroft Shops, *of its lov-
ingly* handcrafted *output, and of the community of Roycrofters, we have included a
facsimile reproduction of*

. . . the Booklet entitled, *THE ROY-
CROFT SHOP: A HISTORY*, as written
by Elbert Hubbard and done into print

PREFACE

by THE ROYCROFTERS, at their shop which is in East Aurora, Erie County, New York, U. S. A., July, MCMVIII.

Sincere thanks go to my children who were enthusiastically involved with this new edition. My gratitude is extended especially to Mr. and Mrs. Charles F. Hamilton for reasons too numerous to mention here—but they know!

NANCY HUBBARD BRADY
House of Hubbard
East Aurora, New York
September 1972

A
THOUSAND
& ONE
EPIGRAMS

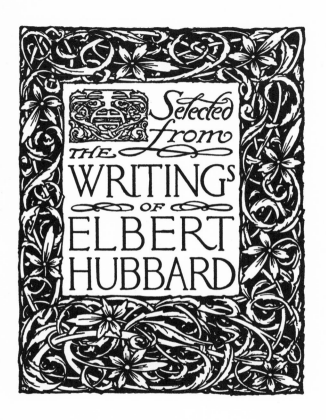

Selected from THE WRITINGS OF ELBERT HUBBARD

A THOUSAND & ONE EPIGRAMS

EVEN the proudest of women are willing to accept orders when the time is ripe; and I am fully convinced that to be domineered over by the right man is a thing all good women warmly desire.

⟿

¶ Fame: To have your name paged by the "buttons" of a fashionable hotel.

⟿

¶ Some howl before they are hurt, others refuse to groan even afterwards.

⟿

¶ Girls should not waste their powder on lobsters. [1]

⟿

¶ Nature will not pi your form as long as you give a clear and clean impression—keep busy! [2]

⟿

¶ Any man who has a job has a chance.

⟿

¶ A failure is a man who has blundered, but is not able to cash in the experience.

¶ When your wife and your affinity are the same person, society has no rope on your foot.

⌐

¶ It takes brains to make money, but any dam fool can inherit. P. S.: I never inherited any money. ⌐

¶ The Buffalo Jones who lassoes an idea and hog-ties it is the only lad who really counts.[3]

⌐

¶ The happiest mortals on earth are ladies who have been bereaved by the loss of their husbands. ⌐

¶ If you lend a willing ear to a man's troubles, you make them your own, and you do not lessen his. ⌐

¶ For while it is still a mooted question whether a man's offspring after the flesh are heirs to his mental and spiritual qualities, it is very sure that the children of his brain are partakers in whatsoever virtue his soul possesses. ⌐

¶ Calvinism has gone, but it had several advantages: for one thing, it gave you peace by supplying a Hell for your rivals and enemies.

¶ To be effective one must be unaffected.

⟞⟝

¶ God and Bwana Tumbo are at variance about big families. We are told that Jesus Christ was God's only begotten son. God believes in quality; Bwana Tumbo wants numbers. [4]

⟞⟝

¶ The sad thing about the optimist is his state of mind concerning himself.

⟞⟝

¶ Literary people of the opposite sex do not really love each other. All they really desire is to read their manuscript aloud to a receptive listener.

⟞⟝

¶ Just how much discord is required in God's formula for a successful life, no one knows; but it must have a use, for it is always there.

⟞⟝

¶ I am not sure just what the unpardonable sin is, but I believe it is a disposition to evade the payment of small bills.

⟞⟝

¶ Fame is delightful, but as collateral it does not rank high.

¶ Every man has moments when he doubts his ability. So does every woman at times doubt her wit and beauty, and long to see them mirrored in a masculine eye. This is why flattery is acceptable. A woman will doubt everything you say except it be compliments to herself—here she believes you are truthful and mentally admires you for your discernment.

¶ Folks who think they are better than others, usually are n't.

¶ Labor is the only prayer that is ever answered.

¶ Man never plots another's undoing except upon the stage. Because you do not like a man is no reason he is your enemy: this is a busy world, and no one has time to sit right down and hate you. The only enemies we have are those we conjure forth from our own inner consciousness. One thing, we are not of enough account; and the idea that a man has enemies is only egotism gone to seed.

¶ Poetry is the bill and coo of sex.

¶ I expect to see the day when the conversational method will be supreme, and teaching will be done practically without books, by object-lessons, thinking things out and doing things.

¶ If men could only know each other, they would never either idolize or hate.

¶ Everything is waiting and watching you to see what signal you hoist from within—you attract that which you desire to attract.

¶ Few people, comparatively, think for themselves.

¶ Men are valuable just in proportion as they are able and willing to work in harmony with other men. When a person loses his ability to co-operate with others, he has joined the Down-and-Out Club.

¶ Several mighty and high church bishops in this country are out against the "new woman." It is noted that they don't say anything against the "old woman" in general or particular.

¶ Drop anchor anywhere and the anchor will drag—that is, if your soul is a limitless, fathomless sea, and not a dog-pound.

¶ The cure for hoodlumism is manual training, and an industrial condition that will give the boy or girl work—congenial work—a fair wage, and a share in the honors of making things. Salvation lies in the Froebel methods carried into manhood.

¶ Too often the reformer has been one who caused the rich to band themselves against the poor.

¶ No performer has a right to do troglodyte stunts except one who can do something else.

¶ Vivisection is blood-lust, screened behind the sacred name of Science.

¶ Success is voltage under control—keeping one hand on the transformer of your Kosmic Kilowatts.

¶ Verily, in the midst of life we are in debt.

¶ Judges demand precedent because they wish to keep in line with public opinion. But public opinion, being a changing entity, is not contained in the things that have gone by, unless society is absolutely at a standstill. Therefore, to get the truth—for truth is that which serves—precedent is the one thing we should avoid.

¶ I do not believe that you can teach a child under fourteen anything by admonition; you do teach him, however, most emphatically by example. If you scold a child, you only add to his vocabulary, and he visits on doll or playfellow your language and manner.

¶ Love is the third rail for Life's Empire State Express.

¶ Man gives little thought to his destination, so long as he can remain out of reach of his pursuer.

¶ And the worst part about making a soldier of a man is not that a soldier kills brown men or white men, but that the soldier loses his own soul.

¶ Blessed is that man who has found his work.

¶ Good people are only half as good, and bad people only half as bad, as other people regard them.

¶ Men do not lack strength; they lack the will to concentrate and act.

¶ If we are ever damned it will not be because we have loved too much, but because we have loved too little.

¶ Force expends itself and dies; every army is marching to its death; nothing but a skull and a skeleton fills helmet and cuirass; the aggressor is overcome by the poison of his pride; victory is only another name for defeat; but the Spirit of Gentleness and Truth is eternal.

¶ Every spirit makes its house, but as afterwards the house confines its spirit, you had better build well.

¶ Nature punishes for most sins, but sacrilege, heresy and blasphemy are not in her calendar, so man has to look after them.

¶ Sing-Sing has several men who were sent there simply because they had Axminster desires and rag-carpet capacities.

⌒

¶ To undertake to supply people with a thing you think they need, but which they do not want, is to have your head elevated on a pike, and your bones buried in the Potter's Field. But wait, and the world will yet want the thing it needs, and your bones may then become sacred relics.

⌒

¶ Lovers are fools, but Nature makes them so.

⌒

¶ I do not want any one to "belong" to me. I would hold my friend only by the virtue that is in my own soul.

⌒

¶ "Should we have an Eleventh Commandment?" asked a youth of the Greatest Living Actress. "Most assuredly, no—we have ten too many now!" answered the divine Sara.

¶ Subscribers not fully understanding my jokes will be supplied laughing-gas at club-rates.

¶ No one knows the vanity of riches save he who has been rich; therefore, I would have every man rich, and I would give every youth a college education that he might know the insignificance of it.

¶ Joyous are the busy, dissatisfied the idle.

¶ Knowledge is the distilled essence of our intuitions, corroborated by experience.

¶ I believe more in the goodness of bad people than I do in the badness of good people.

¶ The poor writers we have always with us— if we take the daily paper.

¶ The blaming of woman for all the ills of the world is the crowning blunder of certain creeds.

¶ Laws that do not embody public opinion can never be enforced.

❡ Abolish fear and you can accomplish whatever you wish.

❡ Talk less and listen more.

❡ Reserve your best thoughts for the elect few.

❡ Idleness is the only sin. A blacksmith singing at his forge, sparks a-flying, anvil ringing, the man materializing an idea—what is finer!

❡ Every tyrant who ever lived has believed in freedom—for himself. Sometimes he has been generous and has been willing to give freedom to a few others whom he deemed fairly intelligent. But freedom for all—nonsense, they would cut themselves with it!

❡ Forbid a man to think for himself or to act for himself and you may add the joy of piracy and the zest of smuggling to his life.

❡ A lie travels by the Marconi route, while Truth goes by slow freight and is often ditched at the first water-tank.

¶ It is opportunity that brings out the great man, but he only is great who prepares for the opportunity—who knows it will come—and who seizes upon it when it arrives.

⌒

¶ Heaven will be very incomplete if all those fine fellows who never lived except in books are not there.

⌒

¶ Gall can never fill a vacuum.

⌒

¶ It is not deeds or acts that last: it is the written record of those deeds and acts.

⌒

¶ Love goes to those who are deserving—not for those who set snares for it and who lie in wait. The life of strife and contest never wins.

⌒

¶ Man, like Deity, creates in his own image. And if you grind all the personality out of a man, and make him but the part of a machine, you are hastening the death of Art, for Art is born of Individuality.

⌒

¶ Love, we say, is life; but love without hope and faith is agonizing death.

¶ I would rather be able to appreciate things I can not have than to have things I am not able to appreciate.

¶ The Divine Economy is automatic and very simple: we receive only that which we give.

¶ Love is an uplift and intoxication: eighty pounds of steam, with the monkeywrench on the blow-off; and the poem you write or the picture you paint is a utilization of the exhaust.

¶ All denominations are needed—they fit a certain type of temperament. Down in Pennsylvania they break up the coal and send it tumbling through various sieves, and each size finds its place in a separate bin. If sects did not serve mankind they would never have been evolved—each sect catches a certain-sized man.

¶ The goal of evolution is self-conquest.

¶ The American girl who marries a foreign duke takes on the management of a jacaseria as a life-job. [5]

¶ It's getting so that it is harder to find a gentleman than a genius.

¶ Art is not a thing: it is a way.

¶ Every man who works in freedom simply reproduces himself. That is what true work is —self-expression, self-revelation.

¶ If any property should be exempt from taxation, it should be all homes that are worth less than three thousand dollars, and not institutions that have big endowments and concerning the necessity of which there is still a question.

¶ Man has constantly grown in power, wisdom, excellence and worth. If he has ever fallen, it has been upstairs, not down.

¶ Happy is the man who conserves his God-given energy until wisdom and not passion shall direct it.

¶ If pleasures are greatest in anticipation, just remember that this is also true of trouble.

¶ Mutual favors do not cancel each other.

¶ Graft is a fool policy.

¶ Most poets die young, not because the gods especially love them, but because life is a bank-account, and to wipe out your balance is to have your checks protested. The excesses of youth are drafts payable at maturity.

¶ I do not read a book: I hold a conversation with the author. I have given as much to Emerson, Schopenhauer, Nietzsche and Whitman as I ever took from them. That they are dead and can not receive my gifts in exchange for theirs is not my fault.

¶ Every life is its own excuse for being, and to deny or refute the untrue things that are said of you is an error in judgment. All wrong recoils upon the doer, and the man who makes wrong statements about others is himself to be pitied, not the man he vilifies. It is better to be lied about than to lie. At the last no one can harm us but ourselves.

¶ If a man has faith in his power, he can wait.

¶ It is a curious fact (or it is n't) that of all the illusions that beset mankind none is quite so curious as that tendency to suppose that we are mentally and morally superior to those who differ from us in opinion.

¶ Nerv. Pros. comes from letting the work chase you; when you chase the work you eat, sleep and laugh; and the man who can do these things is immune from everything.

¶ Any church that is financially and socially prosperous only marks time in ecclesiastical goose-step. It does not advance.

¶ Men who are threatened usually die of old age.

¶ I thank Thee, Lord, that I am as other men are.

¶ An old woman who wants her photograph to look like a coy maiden has forgotten that death is as natural as life.

¶ Nature's best use for genius is to make other men think; to stir things up, so sedimentation does not take place; to break the ankylosis of self-complacency; and start the stream of public opinion running, so it will purify itself.

¶ Sympathy is the first attribute of love as well as its last. And I am not sure but that sympathy is love's own self, vitalized mayhap by some divine actinic ray. Only a thorn-crowned bleeding Christ could have won the adoration of a world. Only the souls who have suffered are well loved. Thus does Golgotha find its recompense. Hark and take courage, ye who are in bonds!

¶ Human hearts are full of love, tenderness and sympathy—hold the right mental attitude and you have the key that unlocks them all. We are afloat on an ocean of Good Will— let down your buckets!

¶ Great organizers are men who are able to distinguish between initiative and "freshness." And quite frequently the difference is very slight.

¶ Great and wise men have ever loved laughter. The vain, the ignorant, the dishonest, the pretentious, alone have dreaded or despised it.

¶ Be wise and teach, but do not punish; for God's in His Heaven, and all's right with the world.

¶ If you can make people kind, not merely respectable, the problem will be solved.

¶ Everybody is interesting when he writes about himself, because he is discussing a subject in which he is vitally interested—whether he understands the theme is another thing.

¶ Forms change, but nothing dies. Everything is in circulation. Men, as well as planets, have their orbits. Some have a wider swing than others, but just wait and they will come back.

¶ Let us all pray to be delivered from whim: it is the poisoner of our joys, the corrupter of our peace, and Dead Sea fruit for all those about us.

¶ Man's greatest blunder has been in trying to make peace with the skies instead of making peace with his neighbor.

¶ Happiness lies in equality.

¶ Get rid of your regrets. You are what you are on account of what you have experienced. And rightly understood, and accepted, all experiences are good, and the bitter ones best of all. I feel sorry for the souls who have not suffered.

¶ Modern business is a most exacting taskmaster. It says, "Thou shalt have no other gods before me." It demands every ounce of energy its devotee has. The thought of a "good time" is not for the businessman. He works and works eternally. He works because he can't stop. And this is the man the Socialists are going to send to the fields!

¶ Friends and credit pursue the man who does not need them.

¶ It's a wise guy who does not monkey with his destiny.

27

❡ If you have no enemies, you are apt to be in the same predicament in regard to friends. ⟜

❡ Everlasting life will be yours if you deserve it—your present belief or disbelief does not affect the issue. But make sure of this: if you are to be a great soul in Heaven, you have got to begin to be a great soul here. ⟜

❡ For the most part, the women who live in history are those who were mismated, misunderstood, neglected, abused, spit upon by Fate, scorned. They were sometimes loved, of course, but loved by those who had no business to love them—loved by the wrong man. But the men who loved them were no more potent factors for good in their evolution than the little men who taunted, harassed, scorned and neglected. ⟜

❡ Let us all take warning, and not begin to prophesy until after the event. ⟜

❡ If your religion does not change you, then you had better change your religion.

¶ Let Health and Wealth be incidental, and you'll have both.

⁓

¶ Hell is a separation, and Heaven is only a going home to our friends.

⁓

¶ Remorse is the form that failure takes when it has made a grab and got nothing.

⁓

¶ If we did not have imagination enough to foresee something better than we now possess, this would be tragedy indeed.

⁓

¶ Every life is its own excuse for being, and should be judged as a whole, not in trivial parts.

⁓

¶ For merit there is a recompense in sneers, and a benefit in sarcasms, and a compensation in hate; for when these things get too pronounced a champion appears.

⁓

¶ Let a man once see himself as others see him, and all enthusiasm vanishes from his heart; and when that is gone he might as well die at once, for enthusiasm is the one necessary ingredient in the recipe for doing good work.

¶ A Miracle: An event described by those to whom it was told by men who did not see it.

⸺

¶ We used to hear much about mere man, but man is now fast growing less mere.

⸺

¶ We work to become, not to acquire.

⸺

¶ Give us the Bough, the Thou and the Jug in right proportion.

⸺

¶ God looked upon His work and saw that it was good. That is where the clergy take issue with Him.

⸺

¶ Hike for Respectability, and cuddle safely under her Paisley, and it's you for a Molly-coddle. Get weaned—in God's name, get weaned!

⸺

¶ Work your grief up into Art, and it is gone.

⸺

¶ Civilization: The matter of wearing your shirt in the confines of your trousers.

⸺

¶ No good sensible working bee listens to the advice of a bedbug on the subject of business.

¶ Education is simply the encouragement of right habits—the fixing of good habits until they become a part of one's nature, and are exercised automatically.

⌐

¶ Many a man's reputation would not know his character if they met on the street.

⌐

¶ Righteousness is simply commonsense; and commonsense is self-interest unlimbered.

⌐

¶ Success is the realization of the estimate which you place upon yourself.

⌐

¶ People who take pains never to do any more than they get paid for, never get paid for any more than they do.

⌐

¶ If you wish to lessen the worries of the world and scatter sunshine as you go, don't bother to go a-slumming, or lift the fallen, or trouble to reclaim the erring—simply pay your debts cheerfully and promptly. It lubricates the wheels of trade, breaks up party ice, gives tone to the social system and liberates good-will.

¶ In the future, the chief duties will consist in so forming one's life as to give the highest possible good, and do the least possible harm to others.

¶ Men who have ideas and express them are yet at bay in the world.

¶ Helpful men are safe men.

¶ Reversing your treatment of the man you have wronged is better than asking his forgiveness.

¶ New Thought offers you no promise of paradise or eternal bliss if you accept it; nor does it threaten you with everlasting hell, if you don't. All it offers is unending work, constant effort, new difficulties; beyond each success is a new trial.

¶ Most reformers wore rubber boots and stood on glass when God sent a current of Commonsense through the Universe.

¶ No great spiritual event befalls those who do not summon it.

¶ If you would have friends, cultivate solitude instead of society. Drink in the ozone, bathe in the sunshine, and out in the silent night, under the stars, say to yourself again and yet again, "I am a part of all my eyes behold!" And the feeling will surely come to you that you are no mere interloper between earth and sky; but that you are a necessary particle of the Whole.

¶ Fear clogs, Faith liberates.

¶ We are all children in the kindergarten of God.

¶ If you would have friends, first learn to do without them.

¶ Life is a search for power. To have power you must have life, and life in abundance. And life in abundance comes only through great love.

¶ Matter is only mind in an opaque condition; and all beauty is but a symbol of spirit.

¶ Do not stand under an umbrella when God rains humor.

❡ Heaven is largely a matter of digestion, and come to think of it digestion is mostly a matter of mind.

❡ Ignorance is not so bad as deception.

❡ I know, I know—Fate has hammered me, too, hammered my soul into better shape than it once was. Relax, cease the struggle, and you have nothing with which to fight.

❡ Life is a sequence and the man who does great work has long been in training for it.

❡ Men become by doing, and the man who holds a gun as a lifework, never becomes anything—not even a part of a machine.

❡ Art is the expression of a man's joy in his work.

❡ Institutions are never much beyond the people—they can not be, for the people dilute everything until it is palatable.

¶ While five o'clock tea may not work, eleven o'clock beer is a roaring success.

⸺

¶ "Who are those who will eventually be damned?" "Oh, the others, the others, the others!"

⸺

¶ There are only two classes of men who live in history: those who crowd a thing to its extreme limit, and those who then arise and cry, "Hold!"

⸺

¶ I modestly protest that simplicity, truthfulness, mental self-reliance, physical health and the education of the hand, as well as brain, shall not be left out of the accounting when we make our formula for a man.

⸺

¶ In all advertising be human. Appeal to the great common instincts of mortal man. Let your advertising speak out of your own personality. And make that personality of yours healthy, normal, sincere and honest.

¶ Educational systems are designed for average intellects.

¶ Life is a bank-account with so much divine energy at your disposal.

¶ I doubt the wisdom of being too wise: and I see much wisdom in some folly.

¶ One can endure sorrow alone, but it takes two to be glad. Only by giving out our joy do we make it our own—by sharing, we double it.

¶ To know all is to forgive all.

¶ Work is for the worker.

¶ I belong to that happy Elect Few who have succeeded in ridding themselves of the friendship of the many.

¶ Fashionable Society is usually nothing but Canned Life. Look out for explosions!

¶ Life is a compromise between fate and free will.

¶ The earth and the fulness thereof belong to the men who can kill; on this rock have Church and State been built.

⌐⌐

¶ High aims are good things, we are told, and doubtless, like the mariners, we should steer our courses by the stars. Still there is good game which lies close to the earth if we knew how to hunt for it—and there is the fun of hunting anyway, game or not.

⌐⌐

¶ As for myself I 'd rather be a good honest wild ass of the desert with long, fuzzy ears, than a poor, imitation bird-of-paradise, stuffed by one hundred and seventeen geniuses.

⌐⌐

¶ Armistices are agreed upon only for the sake of getting into the other's camp to find out what is going on.

⌐⌐

¶ If you suffer, thank God!—it is a sure sign that you are alive.

⌐⌐

¶ Freedom in divorce is the one thing that will transform the marital boor into a gentleman.

⁋ Incompatibility! There is nothing worse!

⁋ Intellectually and morally the fittest have never survived—hence an intellectual race of scrubs.

⁋ Literature is the noblest of all the arts. Music dies on the air, or at best exists only as a memory; oratory ceases with the effort; the painter's colors fade and the canvas rots; the marble is dragged from its pedestal and is broken into fragments; but the *Index Expurgatorius* is as naught, and the books burned by the fires of the *auto da fe* still live. Literature is reproduced ten thousand times ten thousand and lodges its appeal with posterity. It dedicates itself to Time.

⁋ Men who are strong in their own natures are very apt to smile at the good folk who chase the genealogical aniseed trail. It is a harmless diversion with no game at the end of the route.

⁋ Hate was once so thoroughly believed in that we gave it personality and called it the Devil.

¶ Hot air is all right, but see that it is well compressed before you use it.

¶ Not all respectable people are good; and there are many good people who are not respectable.

¶ In most religions there is a strain of ethics, but if religion becomes intense it leaves ethics out of the equation, and then you get a selfishness, a coldness and a cruelty beyond compare.

¶ Innocence is not ignorance: innocence is knowledge and control.

¶ New Thought considers only the user. To "Know Thyself" is all there is of it.

¶ Genius is the ability to act wisely without precedent—the power to do the right thing for the first time.

¶ Music is the only one of the arts that can not be prostituted to a base use.

¶ Intimidation plays a big part in Society under the name of Respectability.

¶ Football occupies the same relation to education that a bullfight does to farming.

¶ Life writes the history upon the face, so that all those who have had a like experience read and understand.

¶ Men are only great as they have sympathy. Imagination is sympathy in motion. And the writers in the United States who possess a universal sympathy, served by a winged imagination, can be counted on the fingers of one hand. We have purists by the score, stylists by the dozen, and advocates by the hundred who defend this, that and the other in strong and splendid English, but they are not men of all-round sympathy.

¶ Hypocrisy is conscious and wilful dishonesty.

¶ Robbers always give much to charity, for thus do they absolve themselves.

¶ To have a full stomach and a fixed income are no small things. However, one may set his mark higher!

¶ Genius consists in snatching success from the jaws of defeat.

¶ My heart goes out to the man who does his work when the "boss" is away, as well as when he is at home.

¶ How hard the tyrants die!

¶ Take your choice: at least an hour's work each day in the open air, or a few weeks every year in bed, looked after by Doctor Jackanapes, with a plumber's bill for a Christmas present.

¶ A ludicro-tragic feature of Chicago Tongue is that those who deal in it most, always are full of grievances and wails because, they allege, other folks are talking about them.[6]

¶ There is a whole round of maladies that can be cured by a new thought, a new sensation, new surroundings. A little excitement or a new experience often clears the cobwebs from the brain.

¶ Humanity is changed as you change environment.

¶ To civilize mankind: make marriage difficult and divorce easy.

¶ Good Philistines make a success of everything they attempt—it is the mental attitude that does it.

¶ There is nothing so hygienic as friendship: Hell is a separation, and Heaven is only going home to your friends.

¶ There is only one thing worth praying for: to be in the line of evolution.

¶ Wisdom does not consist in banishing passion, but in purifying it.

¶ Writers seldom write the things they think. They simply write the things they think other folks think they think.

¶ There was one who thought himself above me, and he was above me until he had that thought.

¶ To fail to win the approval of one's other self is defeat, and there is none other.

¶ This habit of expectancy always marks the strong man. It is a form of attraction: our own comes to us because we desire it; we find what we expect to find, and we receive what we ask for. All life is a prayer—strong natures pray most—and every earnest, sincere prayer is answered.

¶ Those who create beauty are also they who possess it.

¶ It is far safer to trust a normal human heart than a critical, legal mind.

¶ A college degree does not lessen the length of your ears: it only conceals it.

¶ Woman's inaptitude for reasoning has not prevented her from arriving at truth; nor has man's ability to reason prevented him from floundering in absurdity. Logic is one thing and commonsense another.

¶ There are some things that should never be mentioned in polite society—f'r instance, the doings of Polite Society.

❡ I would rather have a big burden and a strong back than a weak back and a caddy to carry life's luggage.

❡ Good healthy egotism in literature is the red corpuscle that makes the thing live. Cupid, naked and unashamed, is always beautiful; we turn away only when some very proper person perceives he is naked and attempts to better the situation by supplying him a coat of mud.

❡ Have n't you ever felt that the prince is as good as the pauper, even if he is no better?

❡ Missionaries are sincere, self-deceived persons suffering from meddler's itch.

❡ I think the reason lawyers have less animosity than preachers or doctors is because their lives are so given up to scraps that no particular scrap really counts.

❡ Good luck is science not yet classified, just as the supernatural is the natural not yet understood.

¶ Now, owls are not really wise—they only look that way. The owl is a sort of college professor.

¶ Habit is the buffer of our feelings, the armor that protects our nerve-force, the great economizer of energy.

¶ Great love-letters are written only to great women.

¶ It is not book-learning young men need, nor instruction about this and that, but a stiffening of the vertebra which will cause them to be loyal to a trust, to act promptly, concentrate their energies: do the thing— "Carry a message to Garcia!" [7]

¶ It is only life and love that give love and life.

¶ Men who sit back and pride themselves on their culture have n't any to speak of.

¶ A retentive memory is a good thing, but the ability to forget is the true token of greatness.

¶ Gossip is only the lack of a worthy theme.

¶ Riches used to take to themselves wings; but nowadays they simply go away in an automobile.

¶ Things that chew the cud do not catch anything.

¶ I love you because you love the things I love.

¶ He who would do a great work must have but one friend—or none.

¶ Do not dump your woes upon people— keep the sad story of your life to yourself. Troubles grow by recounting them.

¶ Be pleasant until ten o'clock in the morning and the rest of the day will take care of itself.

¶ There is a touch of pathos in the thought that while lovers live to make themselves necessary to each other, the mother is working to make herself unnecessary to her children.

¶ To be gentle, generous, lenient, forgiving, and yet never relinquish the vital thing— this is to be great.

¶ This working for a common cause dilutes the sectarian ego, dissolves village caste, makes neighbor acquainted with neighbor, and liberates a vast amount of human love, which otherwise would remain hermetically sealed.

¶ To be popular, hitch your wagon to a lie. Ask Billy Sunday! [8]

¶ The clergy take theirs now; you get yours after you are dead.

¶ To be stupid when inclined and dull when you wish is a boon that goes only with high friendship.

¶ Just why all the cranks in the United States should write me letters, I do not know; but they do. Perhaps there is a sort o' fellow feeling.

¶ Let us wend our way by Love's Welsbach!

¶ It is just as much fun to put fifty dollars in a Savings-Bank as to buy fifty thousand dollars' worth of railroad bonds.

¶ Many a man has busted in business because his necktie did not match his socks.

❡ It is a fortunate wife who can deal with her husband honestly instead of diplomatically.

❡ It is a good policy to leave a few things unsaid.

❡ How far can a woman go to win in Love's race? A step backward is often good policy.

❡ Minimize friction and create harmony. You can get friction, for nothing but harmony costs courtesy and self-control.

❡ It is a great man who, when he finds he has come out at the little end of the horn, simply appropriates the horn and blows it forevermore.

❡ Rogue clients evolve rogue lawyers to do their work; fool patients evolve fool doctors; and superstitious, silly people in the pew secrete a pretentious punk party in the pulpit.

❡ On the other side, where all things are revealed, men wear hats two sizes smaller than here.

¶ He who admits that he, himself, is a worm ought not to complain when he is trodden on.

¶ Requisites for a strong character: bold design, constant practise, frequent mistakes.

¶ No man is free who has not been divorced from popular favor.

¶ When you begin to thirst for knowledge, you drink it in. You need not go out for it nor away. The ocean of it surrounds us as the atmosphere.

¶ It is absurd for a man to make a god of his digestive apparatus, but it is just as bad to forget that the belly is as much the gift of God as the brain.

¶ The selfish wish to govern is often mistaken for a holy zeal in the cause of humanity.

¶ "No man is a hero to his valet." Heroes never have valets.

¶ Priests are not allowed to marry, because if they did, the secrets of the confessional would be called over back fences the next day.

¶ The spiritual and the sensual reach reconciliation in the love of a good woman.

¶ Give us this day our daily work.

¶ Walking delegates usually ride, and never work.

¶ If you talk in your sleep, don't mention my name!

¶ Breathe more, eat less, and think well of everybody—especially doctors.

¶ There is no damnation for any one—there never was, and never will be—and there is no defeat except for those who think defeat. Success is for you. Life is good!

¶ There is no substitute for mother-love. God is that jealous of it that he supplies nothing to equal it.

¶ We always preach about things that are not ours.

¶ It is a herculean task to cope with the handicap of wealth.

¶ When an Anarchist gets a job, buys a lot
and begins to build a home, the "Cause"
has lost him, and can never get him back
for a boutonniere, or just for a ribbon to stick
on his coat. When a Socialist starts a restaurant
and begins to prosper, his Socialistic zeal begins
to lukewarm and his comrades go into mourn-
ing for him as for one who is dead.

⌐

¶ Herbert Spencer deals at length with what
he is pleased to term the "Messianic Idea."
It seems that all nations have ever held the
hope of the coming of a Strong Man, who
would deliver them from the ills that beset
their lives. This hope never dies, although it
assumes different forms, varying according to
conditions. No doubt that the hope that springs
eternal in the United States, when each four
years roll round, is a rudimentary survival of
the Messianic Idea. As yet, however, the
President who is to take the bitterness out
of this cup of life has not been elected.

⌐

¶ If some latter-day skeptics had been among
the twelve apostles, poor Thomas would hardly
have received honorable mention.

¶ Life has sorrows enough of its own without adding to it cats.

¶ The ideas that benefit a man are seldom welcomed by him on first presentation.

¶ East Aurora is not a locality—East Aurora is a condition of mind. [9]

¶ We give explanations to those only who do not ask them.

¶ The wide domain of happiness has never been mapped; but sorrow has been surveyed and known in every part.

¶ It is perfectly safe to say that ninety-nine men out of a hundred, in civilized countries, are opposed to war. We recognize that life is short and the night cometh. Leave us alone!

¶ It is the stupidity of the many that allows one man to bestride the narrow world like a Colossus.

¶ It is the weak man who urges compromise —never the strong man.

¶ It is a well-attested fact that all jokes can be traced back to six originals, evolved in Egypt during the Sixth Dynasty. This being true, it is the right and moreover the duty of every man to improve on any old joke that he may find lying around loose.

⟡

¶ Horatius still stands at the bridge, spear in hand, because a poet placed him there. Paul Revere rides a-down the night, giving his warning cry at every Middlesex village and farm, because Longfellow set the meters in a gallop. Across the waste of waters the enemy calls upon Paul Jones to surrender, and the voice of Paul Jones echoes back, "Damn your souls to hell—we have not yet begun to fight!"

⟡

¶ All success consists in this: You are doing something for somebody—benefiting humanity —and the feeling of success comes from the consciousness of this.

⟡

¶ A criminal: One who does by illegal means what all the rest of us do legally.

❡ Don't be selfish. If you have something that you do not want, and know some one who has no use for it, give it to that person. In this way you can be generous without expenditure or self-denial, and also help another to be the same.

❡ Men do not vary much in virtue: their vices only are different.

❡ If you would have friends, be one.

❡ You should never hurry unless you are in haste.

❡ "I will arise," said the famished Prodigal, "and go to my fodder."

❡ Men and women should commune intellectually—to lovey-dovey is not enough. To lovey-dovey exclusively is to hate afterwards. Where men and women meet only to lovey-dovey, society is essentially barbaric; and where the males monopolize, or think, or pretend to think, that they monopolize wisdom, there is small hope for progress.

⁋ There is no doubt that a teacher once committed to a certain line of thought will cling to that line long after all others have deserted it. In trying to convince others, he convinces himself. This is especially so if he is opposed. Opposition evolves in his mind a maternal affection for the product of his brain, and he defends it blindly to the death. Thus we see why institutions are so conservative. Like the coral insect, they secrete osseous matter; and when a preacher preaches, he himself goes forward to the mourners' bench and accepts all the dogmas that have just been so ably stated.

⁋ Women under thirty seldom know much unless Fate has been kind and cuffed them thoroughly.

⁋ Peace comes to him who brings it, and joy to him who gives it; but a perfect understanding comes to him only who loves perfectly.

⁋ How beautiful that most of our troubles never happen!

⁋ Be severe with nobody but yourself.

⁋ Medical advertisements are not to let you know the disease is curable, but to make you think you have it. Doctors who do not advertise, wish they could.

⁋ Religion is not necessarily kind, considerate, nor sympathetic, but ethics is nothing else.

⁋ God always gives us strength to bear the troubles of each day; but He never calculated on our piling the troubles past, and those to come, on top of those of today.

⁋ I doubt me much that the time will ever come when two pigs, meeting at the trough, will hesitate before jumping into the swill, and the bigger one say to the other, "After you, my dear Alphonse."

⁋ Since "Hamlet" was never equaled, who could have taught its author how to write it?

⁋ It does not take much strength to do things, but it requires great strength to decide on what to do.

¶ No man wins his greatest fame in that to which he has given most of his time: it's his side issue, the thing he does for recreation, his heart's play-spell, that gives him immortality.

¶ It is a great privilege to live, to work, to feel, to endure, to know: to realize that one is the instrument of Deity—being used by the maker to work out His inscrutable purposes.

¶ It is a gross error to suppose that a yellow dog is necessarily nothing but a canine whose capillary covering is highly charged with ocherish pigment.

¶ Nothing is so pleasant as to air our worldly wisdom in epigrammatic nuggets. To sit quiet and listen to another do it—well, that is another matter!

¶ A monarchist believes a monarch should reign; a plutocrat believes in the rule of the rich; a democrat believes that the majority should dictate; an aristocrat thinks only the wise should decide; while an anarchist does not believe in government at all.

¶ Paul going down to Damascus to persecute Christians and coming back one is the true type of the man who grows red in the face over something he does n't know much about.

⌒

¶ How much finer it is to go out in the woods and lift up your voice in song, and be a child, than to fight inclination and waste good God-given energy endeavoring to be proper!

⌒

¶ No woman can be summed up in an algebraic formula, and when a mathematician does a problem to his lady's eyebrow, he forgets entirely that femininity forever equals x.

⌒

¶ Truth, in its struggle for recognition, passes through four distinct stages. First, we say it is damnable, dangerous, disorderly, and will surely disrupt society. Second, we declare it is heretical, infidelic and contrary to the Bible. Third, we say it is really a matter of no imporance either one way or the other. Fourth, we aver that we have always upheld and believed it.

⌒

¶ In this "rushing in" business, keep out, or you may count as one more fool.

¶ Culture consists in getting all your goods into your front windows—and quickly, too.

⌒

¶ That the wealthy and influential class should fear change, and cling stubbornly to conservatism, is certainly to be expected. To convince peacefully this class that spiritual and temporal good can be improved upon by a more liberal policy has been a task a thousand times greater than the exciting of the poor to riot. ⌒

¶ Most of the frightful cruelties inflicted on men during the past have arisen simply out of a difference of opinion arising through a difference in temperament. The question is as live today as it was two thousand years ago: what expression is best? That is, what shall we do to be saved? And concrete absurdity consists in saying we must all do the same thing. ⌒

¶ Don't be a villager—be universal, no matter where you live. ⌒

¶ The only way a woman can ever reform a man is by antithesis. To inspire is something else.

⁋ It is well to remember that, after all, Satan was the first reformer, the first being with a fighting Idea!

⁋ Gentleness and good-cheer — these come before all questions of morals.

⁋ He who does not understand your silence will probably not understand your words.

⁋ The world is full of folks who are quick to ascribe an ulterior motive to every generous act. They ask with uplifted eyebrow: "Was Mary Magdalene sincere? Was n't it just a transient, hysterical spasm of repentance? And about that box of precious ointment— what proof is there that she did n't steal it?"

⁋ The entire Salem Witchcraft insanity was nothing but a bad case of Chicago Tongue. 10

⁋ Progress needs the brakeman, but the brakeman should not spend all his time putting on the brakes.

⁋ Astuteness is only valuable in protecting us from astute people. It adds nothing of value to the community.

¶ Perhaps the friends we have are only our other selves, and we get just what we deserve.

⌒

¶ The expression, "artistic temperament," is often an apologetic term, like "literary sensitiveness," which means that the man has stuck to one task so long and thought in one line so much that he has evolved into just a plain damn fool.

⌒

¶ Attached to the profession of pedagogy is the blighting disgrace of poverty—in other words, its inability to indulge in conspicuous waste and conspicuous leisure. Schoolteaching, not being very respectable, is usually followed by young women until they can get married, or by men until they become lawyers or authors.

⌒

¶ No greater shock ever comes to a young man from the country than the discovery that rich people are, for the most part, woefully ignorant. He discovers that millionaires are too busy making money, and too anxious about what they have made, and their families are too intent upon spending it, to ever acquire a calm, judicial mental attitude.

¶ How sharper than a serpent's tooth is a thankless parent!

¶ An ounce of performance is worth more than a pound of preachment.

¶ You can lead a boy to college, but you can not make him think.

¶ Modern martyrdom is the sweet apotheosis of the things we do not care to avoid.

¶ It is a good policy to leave a few things unsaid.

¶ Self-reliance is very excellent, but as for independence, there is no such thing.

¶ This incapacity for independent action, this moral stupidity, this infirmity of the will, this unwillingness to cheerfully catch hold and lift, are the things that put pure Socialism so far into the future.

¶ There are two kinds of literature: one, the literature of power; and the other, the literature of explanation and apology.

¶ What wonderful things we imagine we would do if we were off on an island somewhere where folks did n't bother so eternally! But why not consider the whole earth an island— a speck—and perform our wonders right here and now?

¶ When one generation comes into possession of the material good that the former generation has gained, and makes that fool remark, "I don't have to work," it straightway is stepping on the chute that gives it a slide to Avernus.

¶ Business is done only where there is enthusiasm. Without good-cheer, firm faith in the future and in your fellow-men, you are a candidate for the Down-and-Out Club.

¶ When war becomes ridiculous instead of splendid, as it surely must some day, our friends at The Hague will have arrived. Hasten the time when Captain Jinks shall be given the laugh.

¶ The doctor and the preacher are modified manifestations of the belief in a vicarious atonement. We look to some one to save us.

¶ I sing the praise of the average woman—the woman who does her work, who is willing to be unknown, who is modest and unaffected, who tries to lessen the pains of earth, and to add to its happiness. She is the true guardian angel of mankind.

¶ Infidels do not revile Christians to the same extent or degree that Christians revile Christians.

¶ Men who marry for gratification, propagation or the matter of buttons and socks, must expect to cope with and deal in a certain amount of quibble, subterfuge, concealments, and double, deep-dyed prevarication. And these things will stain the fabric of the souls of those who juggle them, and leave their mark upon futurity.

¶ In spite of mishap, let the truth stand that those who travel fast and go far, go by Love's Parcel-Post, concerning which there is no limit to the size of the package.

¶ New thoughts are hygienic. Love is a tonic.

¶ Folks who can, do; those who can't, chin.

¶ Men are rich only as they give. He who gives great service gets great returns. Action and reaction are equal, and the radiatory power of the planets balances their attraction. The love you keep is the love you give away.

⌒

¶ I wish to be simple, honest, natural, frank, clean in mind and clean in body, unaffected— ready to say, "I do not know," if so it be, to meet all men on an absolute equality— to face any obstacle and meet every difficulty unafraid and unabashed. I wish to live without hate, whim, jealousy, envy or fear. I wish others to live their lives, too—up to their highest, fullest and best. To that end I pray that I may never meddle, dictate, interfere, give advice that is not wanted, nor assist when my services are not needed. If I can help people, I will do it by giving them a chance to help themselves; and if I can uplift or inspire, let it be by example, inference and suggestion, rather than by injunction and dictation. I desire to Radiate Life!

⌒

¶ The man who does too much leaves himself underdone.

¶ Meanness is more in half-doing than in omitting acts of generosity.

¶ All that glitters is not brass.

¶ Strong men make room for strong men.

¶ Men who sit back and pride themselves on their culture, have n't any to speak of.

¶ Women are all alike in this: they are all different, and most of them are different every hour.

¶ There can be no secret in life and morals, because Nature has provided that every beautiful thought you know and every precious sentiment you feel shall shine out of your face, so that all who are great enough may see, know, understand, appreciate and appropriate. You keep things only by giving them away.

¶ There is no freedom on earth or in any star for those who deny freedom to others.

¶ Not only does beauty fade, but it leaves a record upon the face as to what became of it.

¶ When Li Hung Chang asked Richard Harding Davis if he wrote stories because he was not strong enough to work, he put a question that was quite in order. Li declares that literature should never be a profession, but that every man should write when he hears the "Voice." He himself writes poetry at times, in a meter that is a cross between the style of Steve Crane and that of Yone Noguchi. It is needless to remark that it is great stuff, and Li admits it. [11]

¶ To recognize the accidentally impolitic from the essentially wrong is a step always taken first by a Philistine. The Chosen People damn him for his pains, after which they adopt and swear on their beards that they always held it.

¶ Americans not only fill the teeth of royalty, but we furnish the Old World machinery, ideas and men. For every twenty-five thousand men they supply us, we send them back one, and the one we send them is worth more than the twenty-five thousand they send us.

¶ Our greatest deeds we do unknowingly.

¶ We are not punished for our sins, but by them.

¶ "You say," said the Reno Judge, "that your client was true to one woman?"
"Yes, your Honor; not only was he true to one woman, but more than that—he was true to five, as I can prove."

¶ It is far safer to trust a normal, human heart than a critical, legal mind.

¶ It is life which supplies the writer his theme. People who have not lived, no matter how grammatically they may write, have no message.

¶ It is man who sanctifies a place, and it is work that sanctifies a man.

¶ No man should be pitied except the one who wears his future for a bustle.

¶ Health is potential power. Wealth is an engine that can be used for good if you are an engineer; but to be tied to the flywheel of an engine is rather unfortunate.

❡ You can lead a boy to college, but you can not make him think.

❡ Is it worth while to hate anything—even sin?

❡ The lesson of the Inquisition was worth the price—the martyrs bought freedom for us. The fanged dogs of war, once turned loose upon the man who dared to think, have left as sole successor only a fat and harmless poodle, known as Social Ostracism.

❡ A formal religion is an awful loss to the world, in that it excites the sense of sublimity, and then grounds the wire. The divine passion leads to a prie-dieu when it should lead you to a workbench or "thine easel."

❡ Making men live in three worlds at once—past, present and future—has been the chief harm organized religion has done.

❡ The conduct of lovers is always absurd to the onlookers, but the onlooker has no business to look on: he is a false note in a beautiful symphony, and should be eliminated.

¶ When a man and a woman become absolutely irksome to each other—when their heads are in a different stratum and they breathe a different atmosphere, and have no common ends or ambitions; when they can not sit in silence with each other without positive discomfort; when they grope pathetically for a topic of conversation and never find it; when the deeds of the darkness are remembered with shame in the daylight—then it is time that the State should take its heavy hands off and give the man and woman liberty. Unrelated people give no joy to each other. They never bring out the latent and unsuspected powers that each possess.

¶ Advertising is fast becoming a fine art. Its theme is human wants, and where, when and how they may be gratified. It interests, inspires, educates—sometimes amuses—informs and thereby uplifts and benefits, lubricating existence and helping the old world on its way to the Celestial City of Fine Minds.

¶ In love, unless you are a lobster's hind foot, you eat your cake and keep it, too.

¶ Until now I have had no quarrel with Mr. Bryan of Nebraska, although perhaps I have had reasons. For once upon a hot and dusty day I appeared on the tail-end of a Lake Shore train at Elkhart, Indiana, in an alpaca coat and was loudly cheered by various sweaty persons in overalls. Then other men came, and women, too, and all swore fealty as I shook hands and promised offices. [12]

¶ I hear that New York schoolteachers tell the children that the Devil is loose on Manhattan Isle; and the worst of it is, it's true.

¶ I observe that the new woman still sharpens her lead-pencil with the scissors.

¶ Religions are many and diverse, but reason and goodness are one.

¶ *The Philistine* chastises only those whom it loves. [13]

¶ There recently appeared in the "Revue des Modes" an article with this rather startling headline: "Shall Women Hunt in Pants?" Padmarx says they do now.

❡ Everybody is punk at times. I am, anyway. The desirable thing is not to let the mood become chronic. And then, when the Pivotal Point comes, spread your wings and fly.

❡ The Jew may hang on to a dollar when dealing with the enemy, but he does not dole out pittances to his wife, alternately humor and cuff his children, nor request, by his manner, that elderly people who are not up to date shall get off the earth.

❡ Is there some one who believes in the value of your mission? Ah, I am glad, for without that stimulus you were in a sorry plight. Professor Tyndall once said the finest inspiration he ever received was from an old man who could scarcely read. This man acted as his servant. Each morning the old man would knock on the door of the scientist and call, "Arise, Sir; it is near seven o'clock, and you have great work to do today."

❡ You can not do away with woman by pasting a label on her back reading, "This is only a rag and a bone and a hank of hair."

¶ I think that in Literature the man who wins in the future can not afford to be diffuse or profound. He will be suggestive, and the reader must have the privilege of being learned and profound.

¶ A prig: A person with more money than he needs.

¶ We are moved only by the souls that have suffered and the hearts that know; and so all art that endures is a living, quivering cross-section of life.

¶ A pedant: A person with more education than he can use.

¶ A Pharisee : A man with more religion than he knows what to do with.

¶ Home is where the heart is.

¶ Two-thirds of all preachers, doctors and lawyers are hanging on to the coat-tails of progress, shouting whoa! while a good many of the rest are busy strewing banana-peels along the line of march.

¶ Make use of your friends by being of use to them.

¶ What we microbes think of God does not make much difference to God—we can only mirror ourselves.

¶ A boy is a man in the cocoon; his life is big with winged possibilities.

¶ Life is a warfare—between the sexes.

¶ An author who had many friends, being wise, prayed Setebos to send him an enemy!14

¶ Do not take life too seriously—you will never get out of it alive.

¶ There is no such thing as success in a bad business.

¶ What is the difference between Domestic Science and keeping house? I'll tell you: it's about the same as the difference between securing a pass and accepting the courtesies of the road.

¶ The Law of Compensation never rests, and the men who are taught too much from books are not taught by Deity.

❡ You had better be standard by performance than by pedigree.

❡ The world has always acted on the principle that one good kick deserved another.

❡ Do not lose faith in humanity: there are over ninety million people in America who never played you a single nasty trick.

❡ Fortitude: That quality of mind which does not care what happens so long as it does not happen to us.

❡ Justice: A system of revenge where the State imitates the criminal.

❡ A Conservative: One who is opposed to the things he is in favor of.

❡ The quality of our race turns on the quality of the parents; and especially does the quality of the child turn on the peace, happiness and well-being of the mother. You can not make the mother a disgraced and taunted thing and expect the prógeny to prosper. When you strike a mother, you strike the race.

75

¶ To almost every fond father the idea of discipline is to have the child act just as he does. ◠

¶ Pay the price, and provided you pay the price, the thing you buy is worth the money— no matter what it is. ◠

¶ The world is getting better: to a great degree women have abandoned hoops, bustles, tight shoes, high heels, corsets, hats, gloves, sidesaddles and long skirts; and many there be who a-kneipping go. 15

◠

¶ The more one knows, the more one simplifies. ◠

¶ In order to stand success you must be of a very stern fiber, with all the gods on your side. ◠

¶ If a man has faith in his power he can wait.

◠

¶ It is a fine thing to make yourself needed.

¶ You are what you think, and not what you think you are.

¶ Public speakers are of three kinds: instructive, amusing and punk. The latter predominates.

¶ We should be judged, not by our acts, but by our temptations.

¶ The greatest mistake you can make in this life is to be continually fearing you will make one.

¶ People who need a spiritual adviser, also require a Family Physician.

¶ Things cease to be supernatural when we understand them.

¶ If the boss calls you down be grateful; the probabilities are you should have been fired.

¶ We can stop a Chinaman from coming to the United States; but we can not stop a Chinaman from going to Heaven!

¶ To know you know is power.

¶ When all questions are answered it will be time to telephone the undertaker.

¶ It is more shameful to distrust people than to be deceived by them.

¶ Profanity does not consist in saying damn. Profanity consists in writing it d——n.

¶ A clique is friendship gone to seed.

¶ Life is what you choose to make it.

¶ When a creator of New Thought goes into the business of retailing his product, he often forgets to live it, and soon is transformed into a dealer in Secondhand Thought.

¶ A cabin and God's acre all your own are better than an imitation palace owned by the other fellow.

¶ The man who pursues Pleasure will never catch up with her.

¶ Power gravitates to the man who can use it; and love is the highest form of power that exists.

¶ When Grief is great enough it cuts down until it finds the very soul, and this is Agony. And he who has it does not seek to share it with another, for he knows that no other human being can comprehend it—it belongs to him alone, and he is dumb. There is a dignity and sanctity and grace about suffering; it holds a chastening and purifying quality that makes a king or queen of him who has it. Only the silence of night dare look upon it, and no sympathy save God's can mitigate it.

¶ The average man plays to the gallery of his own self-esteem.

¶ A retentive memory may be a good thing, but the ability to forget is the true token of greatness.

¶ Preserve a right mental attitude — the attitude of courage, frankness and good-cheer. To think rightly is to create.

¶ The average woman sees only the weak points in a strong man, and the good points in a weak one.

¶ Two in a bush is the root of all evil.

❧ Vaccination has not as much in its favor as the belief in witches, nor is it as reasonable, for witchcraft has the endorsement of Scripture.

❧ Chickens always come home to roost, which is right and natural; but when they come home to cackle and crow, that is another matter.

❧ When we get across the River Styx, the first thing we will do is to go behind the ferry-house, and roar us like sucking doves to think that we were born red and died bald and always took the thing so seriously.

❧ Theology is passed along by the law of parental entail. The persistency of the Jew in religious matters is owing in great measure to his filial piety.

❧ Optimism is a kind of heart stimulant— the digitalis of failure.

❧ Violence is transient; hate consumes itself and is blown away by the winds of heaven; jealousy dies; but the righteous thought is a pressure before which malice is powerless.

¶ Dentists were not needed until men began to feed on mush.

¶ In parsing the word, "doormat," it is well to remember that it may be either male or female.

¶ Who is my brother? I'll tell you—he is the one who recognizes the good in me.

¶ When you grow suspicious of a person and begin a system of espionage upon him, your punishment will be that you will find your suspicions true.

¶ Whether genius is transmissible or not is a question, but all authorities agree as to gout.

¶ Do your work with a whole heart and you will succeed—there is so little competition!

¶ When a woman works, she gets a woman's wage; but when she sins she gets a man's pay—and then some.

¶ A Socialist is a man who, so far as he himself is concerned, considers a thing done when he has suggested it.

The age is crying for men; civilization wants men who can save it from dissolution; and those who can benefit it most are those who are freest from prejudice, hate, revenge, whim and fear.

Power knows no evil but the threatened destruction of itself.

When there is a question of success, do not look to this man or that newspaper for help—look to your work, and make it of such a quality that the market must come to you.

You should never go snipe-shooting when there are bears in sight.

Poor people usually mind other people's business, and therefore have no business of their own.

The reward of a good deed is to have done it.

When sympathy finds vent in vengeance and love takes the form of strife, who can say where it will end?

Be yourself.

¶ The author who has not made warm friends and then lost them in an hour by writing things that did not agree with the preconceived ideas of those friends, has either not written well or not been read. Every preacher who preaches ably has two doors to his church: one where he attracts people in and the other through which he preaches them out. Still there is recompense in the thought that people who walk out with unnecessary clatter are often found after many moons tiptoeing in again. Yet I do not see how any man, though he be divine, could hope, or expect, to have as many as twelve disciples for three years and not be denied, doubted and betrayed. If you have thoughts and speak them frankly, Golgotha for you is not far away.

¶ Power manifests itself in conspicuous waste, and the habit grows until conspicuous waste imagines itself power.

¶ You must not only bury your dead, but you must forget where, smoothing every grave —else you are not safe from ghosts—ghosts, my fine sir!

¶ You can't get away from yourself by going to a booze-bazaar.

¶ The house can get along without you all right; but if you are really on to your job, the house will never think so.

¶ To have many friends, and then when calumny lowers, or calamity threatens, to have these friends suddenly desert you— what happier fate?

¶ To know but one religion is not to know that one.

¶ To know the right woman is a liberal education.

¶ To know when to be generous and when firm—this is wisdom.

¶ There is no moment that comes to mortals so charged with peace and precious joy as the moment of reconciliation. The ineffable joy of forgiving and being forgiven forms an ecstacy that might well arouse the envy of the gods.

¶ Our greatest deeds we do unknowingly.

¶ Say what you will of the coldness and
selfishness of men, at the last we long for
companionship and the fellowship of our kind.
We are lost children, and when alone and the
darkness begins to gather, we long for the
close relationship of the brothers and sisters
we knew in our childhood, and cry for the
gentle arms that once rocked us to sleep. We
are homesick amid this sad, mad rush for
wealth and place and power. The calm of the
country invites, and we fain would do with
fewer things, and go back to simplicity and
rest.

¶ Sincerity without sympathy is devilish;
learning without pity is to be avoided; education without humor is preposterous.

¶ Of all examples of blind imbecility on
part of men, none is so preposterous as the
opinions men hold of other men. Genius does
not recognize genius; worth is blind to worth.
Men often taunt women with treating other
women unjustly, but the records of great men
who have scorned other great men leave the
injustice of woman towards woman quite
out of the race.

¶ Live truth instead of professing it.

¶ Give us this day our daily work.

¶ Vivisection is blood-lust, screened behind the sacred name of Sympathy.

¶ Don't sit down in the meadow and wait for the cow to back up and be milked—go after the cow.

¶ We are traveling to the Beautiful City of the Ideal, and all good work done is a report of our progress.

¶ An American Religion: Work, play, breathe, bathe, study, live, laugh and love.

¶ The man who refers to his wife as "excess baggage" is rude, vulgar and lacking in the esthetic instinct.

¶ It requires a Pharaoh to develop a Moses, just as it took a George the Third to evolve George Washington. Blessed be stupidity!

¶ A creed is an ossified metaphor.

¶ Expectancy is an exciting interval between rounds.

¶ We are under bonds for the moderate use of every faculty, and he who misuses any of God's gifts may not hope to go unscathed.

¶ The blessing that is compulsory is not wholly good, and any system of morals which has to be forced on us is immoral.

¶ A renunciant is like a man who can not dance—he is jealous of the joyous.

¶ The greatest joy in life is the joy of being "next."

¶ We become robust, only through exercise, and every faculty of the mind and every attribute of the soul grows strong, only as it is exercised. So you had better exercise your highest and best only, else you may give strength to habits and inclinations that may master you, to your great disadvantage.

¶ He is a great man who accepts the lemons that Fate hands out to him and uses them to start a lemonade-stand.

¶ Dignity is not valuable until you forget that you have it.

¶ Personally I like the rogue—he is most companionable, especially if you have no work to do.

¶ Young women with ambitions should be very crafty and cautious, lest mayhap they be caught in the soft, silken mesh of a happy marriage, and go down to oblivion, dead to the world.

¶ Your friend is the man who knows all about you, and still likes you.

¶ Weak people are either good or crafty. Only strength is frank.

¶ Pushing to the front is very bad. You had better get in line and await your turn, then you won't evolve a rhino spiritual rind and grow a crop of bristles up and down your back.

¶ The delight of creative work lies in self-discovery—you are mining nuggets of power out of your own cosmos, and the find comes as a great and glad surprise.

❡ Jael hit the nail on the head. Then she turned, adjusted her Marcel Wave, and with a satirical laugh said, "And he, like the rest of 'em, was always shouting about a woman not being able to drive a nail!"

❡ Women are all alike in this: they are all different, and most of them are different every hour.

❡ Be from Missouri, of course; but for God's sake forget it occasionally.

❡ Life without absorbing occupation is hell —joy consists in forgetting life.

❡ To go fast, go slow.

❡ To be true to your own is the natural thing, because it is the right thing.

❡ To eliminate the needless and to keep the good is the problem of progress.

❡ To give a list of the great artists that the world has seen would be to name a list of lovers.

¶ The brain needs exercise as much as the body, and vicarious thinking is as erroneous as vicarious exercise.

¶ Seek, and ye shall find: knock, and nothing shall be opened unto you.

¶ We can never have a noble race of men until we have a noble race of mothers.

¶ The man who married a manicurist, still gets his nails pared downtown.

¶ A man thinks (sometimes), but a woman gives a function.

¶ We grow by doing, not by thinking of our thoughts and feeling of our feelings.

¶ The optimist is like a bear that hibernates —it dines off its adipose.

¶ Babies are the dice of destiny.

¶ Judge Landis rules that the lady who exploits her husband's trousers is only entitled to the use of one-third of the find.

❡ The modest woman is the one who cries her wares in an artistic and effective manner.

❡ We help ourselves only as we help others.

❡ Do not aspire to be king of the Belliakers —there's too much competition for the place.

❡ A disciple is a man who does not understand. He thinks that he is on, but he is n't. The true token of the disciple is that he is quite willing to let the other man do all the thinking.

❡ If you are without hope you are without fear.

❡ Piety is the tinfoil of pretense.

❡ The grouch gets nothing but a cold in the head. Keep sweet!

❡ Push forward to success, like an actress followed by a stage-door Johnny.

❡ The young man who can smoke cigarettes or leave them alone is the first one to be laid off when the panic comes.

¶ The soul grows by leaps and bounds, by throes and throbs. A flash! and a glory stands revealed for which you have been blindly groping through the years.

⌒

¶ Every sanitarium, every hotel, every public institution—every family, I was going to say —has two lives: the placid, moving life that the public knows, and the throbbing, pulsing life of plot and counterplot—the life that goes on beneath the surface. It is the same with the human body: how bright and calm the eye, how smooth and soft the skin, how warm and beautiful this rose mesh of flesh! But beneath there is a seething struggle between the forces of life and the forces of disintegration—and eventually nothing succeeds but failure.

⌒

¶ People whose souls are made of dawnstuff and starshine may make mistakes, but God will not judge them by these alone.

⌒

¶ If you have ceased to be moved by religious emotion, no longer dwell on poetry, and are not swayed by music, it is because the love instinct in you has withered to ashes of roses.

¶ Platonic love is the only kind of love that is blind. It never knows where it is going to fetch up.

¶ Bees have a scheme whereby they eliminate the useless drones. That is where the bees set man a pace. But bees have no way of making a worker out of a drone; and possibly that is where we score one on Brer Bee.

¶ The man who lives truth, if such there be, does not think it worth while to formulate it. He knows no more of truth than the fishes know of the sea. It is the gyve and the fetter that make a man formulate truth. Only prisoners meditate. And so does the philosopher forever meditate upon plans of escape—escape from his own limitations, and the bonds of custom, prejudice, ignorance and pride.

¶ We know that work is a blessing, that Winter is as necessary as Summer, that night is as useful as day, that death is a manifestation of life, and just as good. We believe in the Now and Here. We believe in You, and we believe in a Power that is in ourselves that makes for Righteousness.

¶ That affinity business, like politics, makes strange bedfellows.

¶ When a man retires from business, God takes his word for it and soon tosses him into the hell-box.

¶ A discreet ignorance is a part of every good woman's education. Bona-fide ignorance is quite another thing; and this seems a case where the spurious is more valuable than the genuine.

¶ The married man who wants a change of venue is probably headed for the divorce-court.

¶ Morality is the formaldehyde of theology.

¶ Positive anything is better than negative nothing.

¶ When trouble comes, wise men take to their work: weak men take to the woods.

¶ A college degree is a social certificate, not a proof of competence.

¶ Your own will come to you, if you hold the thought firmly and—hustle.

¶ The millennium will be here when Washington, D. C., goes dry.

¶ You can often tell a college graduate by the fact that when he goes to the theater he takes along some vegetables and a bean-blower.

¶ The nickelodeon is for folks who have nowhere else to go, but home.

¶ The man who marries a model housekeeper has more trouble than the hobo who reported, "One empty going East!"

¶ Love Art wisely, but not too well, or it's you for a dope-fiend.

¶ We make our money out of our friends—our enemies will not do business with us.

¶ A disciple is an individual who is hotly intent on hitching his ice-wagon to a star.

¶ Happiness lies in self-forgetfulness.

¶ Wealth is an engine that can be used for power if you are an engineer; but to be tied to the flywheel of an engine is rather a misfortune.

¶ The sense of separateness is Hell.

¶ Young man, don't get groggy over girls, religion, words, art or politics. They are all good in moderation, but bad if you get an overdose.

¶ We are brothers not only to all who live, but to all who have gone before.

¶ A conservative is a man who is too cowardly to fight, and too fat to run.

¶ The finger of Time needs the service of a manicure.

¶ Respectability is the dickey on the bosom of civilization.

¶ The balsam to the pungent fact that the truth hurts is the soothing knowledge that 't is seldom told.

❡ Laughter is the solace of the sad.

❡ Mind your own business, and thus give other folks an opportunity to mind theirs.

❡ There is nothing so good as the sun and the wind for driving the foolishness out of one.

❡ Art is the uplifting of the beautiful so that all may see and enjoy.

❡ The only right you need is the right to be useful.

❡ Think twice before you speak and then talk to yourself.

❡ To be famous is to be slandered by people who do not know you.

❡ If you would be happy let not happiness be your aim.

❡ A bluejay in the bush is worth two on a woman's bonnet.

❡ People fit for self-government have it. Independence in men or nations is an achievement, not a bequest.

¶ Levitation: The creeping up of your trousers when you ride horseback, so that they supply you a necktie.

⌐

¶ To loom up large in life, get close to the camera. ⌐

¶ Charity suffereth long — and so does the man who tries to live on it.

⌐

¶ A good lie for its own sake is ever pleasing to honest men, but a patched-up record never.

⌐

¶ The original noise is what counts — most people are merely echoes.

⌐

¶ The man who makes the deepest notches on the Stick of Time is not usually preceded by a brass band. ⌐

¶ Loneliness consists in enduring the presence of one who does not understand.

⌐

¶ Imagination is sympathy illumined by brains.

¶You had better learn to accept all the small misfits and the trivial annoyances of life as a matter of course. To allow them to receive attention beyond their deserts is to wear the web of your life to the warp. Be on the lookout for the great joys, and never let mosquitoes worry you into a passion.

¶When the many advise you what you can not afford to miss in the way of a book, you can safely let it alone.

¶The only sin is to be unkind.

¶It is not art but heart that wins, the wide world over.

¶A duty is a pleasure which we try to make ourselves believe is a hardship.

¶Public opinion is the judgment of the incapable many opposed to that of the discerning few.

¶Power unrestrained is always tragic. The world is held in place by the opposition of forces.

¶ When we remember that hoarse guttural cry of "Away with Him! Away with Him!" and when we recall that some of the best and noblest men that ever lived have been reviled and traduced, indicted and executed by so-called good men—certainly men who were sincere—how can we open our hearts to the tales of discredit told of any man?

¶ Who ever saw a tightwad that was n't poor?

¶ Urge your own spontaneous thought against all prudential considerations, and the world will believe in you, or hate you—the difference is small.

¶ There are three kinds of friends: those who love you; those who are indifferent to you; and next friends, these being the people who want something that is yours.

¶ There are two kinds of thought: New Thought and Secondhand Thought. New Thought is made up of thoughts you, yourself, think. The other kind is supplied to you by jobbers.

¶ It is foolish to say sharp, hasty things, but 't is a deal more foolish to write 'em. When a man sends you an impudent letter, sit right down and give it back to him with interest ten times compounded—and then throw both letters in the wastebasket.

⌒

¶ Most poets think the scissors of Fate has them cut to write poetry.

⌒

¶ Would you have your name smell sweet with the myrrh of remembrance and chime melodiously in the ear of future days, then cultivate faith, not doubt, and give every man credit for the good he does, never seeking to attribute base motives to beautiful acts. Actions count.

⌒

¶ A man is as good as he has to be, and a woman as bad as she dares.

⌒

¶ All who feel free to hike when the weather gets thick would do well to get in line with the policy of the house.

¶ The only way a woman can really manage a man is by obeying him.

¶ A woman can defend her virtue from men, much more easily than she can protect her reputation from women.

¶ He who doeth his work and cutteth out the gabfest shall on the Great Day of Readjustment, stand in.

¶ A civil tongue and a deaf ear mean money in the bank.

¶ Verily the most necessary thing in a shop, store, bank, railroad-office or factory is to keep the peace.

¶ Punishment should fit the criminal, not the crime.

¶ A dead fish will float downstream, but it takes a live one to swim against the current.

¶ Most of us are too polite to tell the truth.

¶ Chase your work or your work will chase you.

¶ The Psalmist speaks of something that "passeth the love of woman"; but the Psalmist was wrong—nothing does.

⸺

¶ Success consists in the climb.

⸺

¶ Paternity is a more or less important office, I will admit, but since it does not involve danger, risk, courage, self-sacrifice or heroism, it can not compare with maternity.

⸺

¶ If you want work well done, select a busy man—the other kind has no time.

⸺

¶ The reason the Goddess is blindfolded is so she can not see what the lawyers and judges do, for if she did she would fall dead.

⸺

¶ Difficulties afford heroism its opportunity. Blessed be difficulty!

⸺

¶ The joy of living is to watch the death of things. Note the happiness of the funeral fiend.

⸺

¶ The lawyer is a privateer; the thief is a pirate. One gets a knighthood, the other a rope.

¶ A man is always better than his creed, unless perchance he makes up a new one every day.

¶ Knowledge consists in having a stenographer who knows where to find the thing.

¶ An Optimist: A neurotic person with gooseflesh, and teeth a-chatter, trying hard to be brave.

¶ Law: A scheme for protecting the parasite and prolonging the life of the rogue, averting the natural consequences which would otherwise come to them.

¶ God will not look you over for medals, degrees or diplomas, but for scars.

¶ Philistines do not believe in the Devil—they spell evil backward and put it in capitals, thus: LIVE!

¶ Poise, Patience, Love—these are the touchstones that surmount obstacles.

¶ They who live by the hammer shall die by the hammer.

❡ A sincere man: One who bluffs only a part of the time.

❡ The outcome of the battle is of no importance—but, how did you fight?

❡ The people who taunt other people with having taken temporary refuge in a pig-pen are usually those who live in pig-pens the whole year round.

❡ The popular plan to gain freedom is to enslave others.

❡ Imagination: Taking the halter off your thoughts and giving them a good kick behind.

❡ Every knock is a boost.

❡ Gratitude: A lively sense of anticipation concerning favors about to be received.

❡ To have friends—be one.

❡ The Law of Consequences works both ways: by associating with the sinner and recognizing the good in him, you unconsciously recognize the good in yourself.

¶ A College Degree is a Social Certificate, not a proof of competence.

¶ The man who does not know, and is not afraid to say so, is in the line of evolution.

¶ A committee is a thing which takes a week to do what one good man can do in an hour.

¶ You should always have some one to help you keep a secret.

¶ Most people who pride themselves on riding a hobby don't—the hobby is in the saddle.

¶ There is every reason to believe that Atlas was a college graduate who had just received his degree.

¶ A live language has no grammar; dead ones have.

¶ The orator who can not introduce himself can not do as much for his subject.

¶ It's tough to be a has-been, but to be a never-was is fierce.

¶ I know a man who got a liberal education while waiting for his wife to put on her hat.

¶ The opposition towards great men is right and natural: it is a part of Nature's plan to hold the balance true, "lest ye become as gods!"

¶ People who tell hard-luck stories always have hard-luck stories to tell.

¶ The one unethical thing in the universe is to "brand" any one with a bad name, especially so if this person happens to be in the same line of business as yourself; because none of us is unprejudiced where our interests are concerned. The business world no longer knocks on a competitor.

¶ Degeneracy always begins in the cities; and the failure of civilization has come when the cities succeed and the urbanites decline.

¶ The object of teaching a child is to enable him to get along without his teacher.

¶ Idleness is the disgrace, not busy-ness.

¶ He alone is immune from cephalo-genesis who has butted the wall three times and perceived that it fell not. [16]

⚬

¶ Oratory: Chin-music with Prince Albert accompaniment. ⚬

¶ The safe man is the man who is on intimate terms with one woman and no more.

⚬

¶ The man of violence has ever received quick recognition, but not a lasting fame. We deify only the Gentle Man—the man of thought and feeling—the man of heart. The sober good sense of the time, simply through the law of self-preservation, will not continue to push to the front the man who delights in a fight. ⚬

¶ If people have wronged you, it will do no harm to give them a chance to forget it.

⚬

¶ The men of genius have often been the sons of commonplace parents—no hovel is safe from it. ⚬

¶ A mob is made up of cotton waste saturated with oil, and a focused idea causes spontaneous combustion.

¶ Anarchy, being disorganization, means the quick return to tyranny, through the rule of the strong man who arises in his lust for power and takes command by right of might at the psychologic moment.

¶ Logic: An instrument used for bolstering a prejudice.

¶ According to the Mosaic account, woman was a sort of side-issue.

¶ The man of genius conceives things; the man of talent carries them forward to completion.

¶ The man intent on saving his soul has already lost his. The Devil has him, body and boots.

¶ Anchorage is what most people pray for, when what we really need is God's great open sea.

¶ The pigmy party thinks he is being sat on or held back. Forget it! Nothing can hold a man back but his own limitations.

¶ All progress begins with a crime.

❡ The most helpful symptom in the business world today is that business people are realizing that you can not pauperize people without making them paupers.

❡ As a career, the business of an orthodox preacher is about as successful as that of a celluloid dog chasing an asbestos cat through Hell.

❡ No man with whiskers should ever be allowed to run an automobile or to ride in one.

❡ Get out or get in line.

❡ The more harmony you possess, the stronger you are.

❡ Faith is a fog—knowledge is seeing.

❡ The average honeymoon is merely a spilling of the molasses cruet.

❡ The more points at which you touch humanity, the greater your influence.

¶ If the Devil finds you idle he will set you to work as sure as Hell.

——

¶ The woman who boasts of her virtue is one who probably was tested at an inopportune time by the wrong man.

——

¶ The more discord you have in your own cosmos, the weaker you are—you are that much nearer death and dissolution.

——

¶ Success: A subtle connivance of Nature for bringing about a man's defeat.

——

¶ The mintage of wisdom is to know that rest is rust, and that real life lies in Love, Laughter and Work.

¶ Recipe for trouble: Take a little of nothing, and then put in some more nothing and stir up. Flavor with fear, a jigger of grouch, a piece of lemon, and serve hot to those nearest.

——

¶ Caste in society is a result of uric acid in the ego.

——

¶ Let us pity the folks who are not here.

¶ Wisdom: A term Pride uses when talking of Necessity.

¶ All exclusive friendships breed factions and feuds, and tend in the end to separate people.

¶ Death: A readjustment of life's forces.

¶ The longing for perpetual bliss, in perfect peace, where all good things are provided, might well seem a malevolent inspiration from the Lords of Death and Darkness. We grow only by enduring and overcoming.

¶ And remember this: Yesterday's successes belong to yesterday, with all of yesterday's defeats and sorrows. The day is Here. The time is Now.

¶ The individual who has not known an all-absorbing love has not the spiritual vision that is a passport to Paradise.

¶ The last word is this: Nothing matters, and no difference what happens, the end is well. But wisdom consists in hustling just the same.

¶ A man who owns real estate owns up in the air and down in the earth quite a ways. If his lot is only twenty-five by one hundred on the surface, there is compensation in the fact that it is four thousand miles thick and five thousand miles high. A Chinaman can resist him legally if he goes more than four thousand miles down, but no angel cares how high he soars. And it is a curious fact to the student of things that man has not only parceled out the earth, but in doing so has given title to the air. My attorney tells me that no man has a legal right to sail his balloon over my premises without my permission, and further than that, I can warn him off and then apprehend him for trespass. In fact, when aeronautics are perfected, it will give rise to a whole new round of law business as to rights of way, keeping to the right, collisions, flying without lights, etc. Let lawyers take heart.

¶ Orthodoxy is a corpse that does not know it is dead.

¶ The human race must be Burbanked before we will ever have a noble race of men and women.

¶ The probable fact is that we are descended not only from monkeys but from monks.

¶ The mind sees all, hears all, listens, sifts, weighs and decides. Over against this there is something in man which sees the mind and watches its workings—which analyzes the mind and knows why it does certain things, which knows the mind is not the soul; and this something that knows the mind is not the soul, is the soul.

¶ Grammar is the grave of letters.

¶ Live each day so as to shake hands with yourself every night.

¶ The man who sees a need is the one to supply it.

¶ The man who is worthy of being a leader of men will never complain of the stupidity of his helpers, of the ingratitude of mankind, nor of the inappreciation of the public. These things are all a part of the great game of life, and to meet them and not go down before them in discouragement and defeat is the final proof of power.

¶You can always tell an inspired book by its Oxford binding. ◄►

¶The man who gets just as much fun in putting two dollars in the bank as in spending it is a financier. ◄►

¶As a matter of choice, platonic love is better than plutonic.

◄►

¶All strong men begin by worshiping at a shrine, and if they continue to grow they shift their allegiance until they know only one altar and that is the Ideal which dwells in their own hearts. ◄►

¶The greatest enemy of progress the world has ever seen has been the Religious Trust.

◄►

¶Cultivate only those habits that you are willing should master you.

◄►

¶A soldier is a slave—he does what he is told to do—everything is provided for him—his head is a superfluity. He is only a stick used by men to strike other men; and he is often tossed to Hell without a second thought.

◄►

¶As a man thinketh, so is she.

¶ Polygamy: An endeavor to get more out of life than there is in it.

¶ An idea that is not dangerous is unworthy of being called an idea at all.

¶ The history of the Church is a history of endeavor to keep it from drifting into the thing it professes not to be—concrete selfishness.

¶ Every man is a damn fool for at least five minutes every day. Wisdom consists in not exceeding the limit.

¶ A man is always better than his creed, unless perchance he makes a new one every day.

¶ The habit of borrowing small sums of money—anticipating pay-day—is a pernicious practise and breaks many a friendship. It is no kindness to loan money to a professional borrower.

¶ All that tends to tyranny in parents manifests itself in slavish traits in the children. Freedom is a condition of mind, and the best way to secure it is to breed it.

¶ All things work together for good, whether you love the Lord or not.

¶ There are six requisites in every happy marriage. The first is Faith and the remaining five are Confidence.

¶ Nature in her endeavors to keep man well has not only to fight disease, but often the doctor as well.

¶ The man who borrows takes things easier than the one who lends.

¶ The greatest thing in the world is joy, but only the stricken know this.

¶ All suffering is caused by an obstacle in the path of a force. See that you are not your own obstacle.

¶ Culture is only culture when the owner is not aware of its existence. Capture culture, hog-tie it, and clap your brand upon it, and you find the shock has killed the thing you loved. You can brand a steer, but you can not brand deer.

¶ Men in gym suits are all on an equality.

¶ All separations of society into sacred and secular, good and bad, saved and lost, learned and illiterate, rich and poor, are illusions which mark certain periods in the evolution of society.

¶ A school should not be a preparation for life. A school should be life.

¶ Don't try to eliminate the old-fashioned virtues—many have tried it with indifferent success. No good substitute has yet been found for simplicity, frankness, sobriety, industry and sincerity.

¶ The Great Big Black Things that have loomed against the horizon of my life, threatening to devour me, simply loomed and nothing more. The things that have really made me miss my train have always been sweet, soft, pretty, pleasant things of which I was not in the least afraid.

¶ Co-operation, not competition, is the life of business.

¶ Don't get your headlight behind: reminiscence means stagnation.

¶ Cupid anticipated Marconi.

118

¶ Atlas could never have carried the world had he fixed his thought on the size of it.

¶ The gossip of women is usually of a patty-pan order and comparatively harmless compared with that of men.

¶ Do not separate yourself from plain people; be one with all—be universal.

¶ Constancy, unswerving and eternal, is only possible where men and women are free.

¶ The finest friendships are between those who can do without each other.

¶ As a man grows in experience his theories of conduct become fewer.

¶ Confirmed bachelors are those who have been confirmed by a woman.

¶ Do not keep your kindness in water-tight compartments. If it runs over a bit 't will do no harm.

¶ Discontent is inertia on a strike.

¶ A little more patience, a little more charity for all, a little more devotion, a little more love; with less bowing down to the past, and a silent ignoring of pretended authority; a brave looking forward to the future with more faith in our fellows, and the race will be ripe for a great burst of light and life.

¶ Fear is a ptomaine, but love is a panacea.

¶ The cities may have their little mobs and riots, but the farmers will plow and sow and reap and feed their stock, and go forth to their labors until the evening. The farmers have ever and always been the hope of the world.

¶ A goodly dash of indifference is a requisite in the formula for doing a great work.

¶ The Church saves sinners, but Science seeks to stop their manufacture.

¶ The cure for imaginary ills is a genuine one.

¶ The man who can smile at his defeat has won.

¶ A Pessimist is one who has been intimately acquainted with an Optimist.

¶ Every quarrel begins in nothing and ends in a struggle for supremacy.

¶ A person with strength of character is one who has strong feelings, and strong command over them.

¶ The businessman is the man who gets the business.

¶ Heaven is largely a matter of digestion.

¶ God must dearly love the fools, otherwise He would never have made so many of us.

¶ People who are not up on a thing are usually down on it.

¶ The Red Light is neither a place nor a location—it is a condition of mind.

¶ To know the worst is peace—it is uncertainty that kills.

¶ The fanged dogs of war, once turned loose upon the man who dared to think, have left as sole successor only a fat and harmless poodle, known as Social Ostracism.

¶ Competition has been so general that economists mistook it for a Law of Nature, when it was only an incident.

¶ Let what thou hearest in the house of thy friend be as if it were not.

¶ Before co-operation comes in any line, there is always competition pushed to a point that threatens destruction and promises chaos; then to avert ruin, men devise a better way, a plan that conserves and economizes, and behold it is found in co-operation.

¶ The fact that a man advertises, does not prove that man's inability to do work of a high grade, any more than you can assume that because a man does not advertise he is safe and competent.

¶ Art is sex emotion, captured and organized.

¶Art is the blossoming of the soul. We can not make the plant blossom; all we can do is to comply with the conditions of growth.

⸺

¶Do not go out of your way to do good, but do good whenever it comes your way.

⸺

¶The facts we get out of work have glue on them; but the facts we get out of books are greased. ⸺

¶Clothes play a most important part in Cupid's pranks. Though the little god himself goes naked, he never allows his votaries to follow suit. ⸺

¶Art is not a thing separate and apart; art is only the best way of doing things.

⸺

¶The gossip microbe is born of vacuity and breeds in idle minds.

⸺

¶Do not go up against another man's game: get a game of your own and play it to the limit. And by the way, a game where both parties do not win is immoral.

❡ Orators, people asleep, women in the toilet-room of a Pullman car, know nothing of the flight of time.

❡ A people who give women the right to soak themselves with strong drink, and yet withhold the right of women to say whether the temptation shall be perpetuated; who pray for rain; for fair winds; for success in battle, and that Deity shall interpose and confound the knavish tricks of commercial competitors, should not be blamed if their actions and ideals do not always co-operate.

❡ Be careful how you manage men, for the day is surely coming when, if you have not love and yet attempt to manage men, you will pay for your rashness with your life.

❡ A vast number of men and women see the fact that immunity and exemption are not desirable, that nothing can ever be given away, and that something for nothing is very dear.

❡ A what-not education may be impressive, but it is worthless as collateral.

¶ A good habit is a lubricant that reduces the friction of life to a point where progress is possible.

¶ Be a mixer, but don't get mixed.

¶ The choice between a miter and a helmet is nil, and when the owner converses through his headgear, his logic is alike vulnerable and valueless.

¶ Kiss your baby on the top of his head, and let no one kiss him anywhere else. Grown-ups can kiss each other where they are invited —that's their privilege.

¶ The business of the orator is to inspire other men to think and act for themselves.

¶ A woman may admire, respect, revere and obey, but she does not love until a passion seizes upon her that has in it the abandon of Niagara.

¶ Enjoy what you have, work for what you lack.

¶ Civilization is the expeditious way of doing things.

¶ A preacher is Society's Walking Delegate. He is the self-appointed business agent of divinity, and no contract between God and man, man and man, or man and woman is valid unless ratified by him. All who do not belong to his Union are scabs!

¶ Caste is a Chinese Wall that shuts people in as well as out.

¶ The essence of power lies in reserve; but it is well to remember that grouch and reserve are not the same.

¶ All my gods dwell in temples made with hands.

¶ Depend upon it, the best antiseptic for decay is an active interest in human affairs: Those live longest who live most.

¶ The entire Christian doctrine of rewards and punishments, of a vicarious atonement and the substitution of a pure and holy man for the culprit, is a vicious and misleading philosophy.

¶ Carry your chin in and the crown of your head high. We are gods in the chrysalis.

⌐

¶ Appreciation of the worthy can come only from those who are not unworthy.

⌐

¶ The English go about with the chip of peace upon their shoulders.

⌐

¶ Dame Justice is sometimes said to be blind, but only in one eye.

⌐

¶ All literature is advertising. And all genuine advertisements are literature.

⌐

¶ The duels between our celestial and terrestrial natures often take place at so deep a point in our souls that we are not aware of the conflict—but still the fight is on.

⌐

¶ Calm, patient, persistent pressure wins. It wins! Violence is transient. Hate, wrath, vengeance are all forms of fear, and do not endure. Silent, persistent effort will dissipate them all. Be strong!

¶ A parody is a calico cat stuffed with cotton.

¶ Barbaric people prize gold and make much use of silver. But the consumption of iron is the badge of civilization.

¶ The business of government is to make all government unnecessary, just as wise parents are bringing up their children to do without them.

¶ Any man in any walk of life, who puts jealousy, hate and fear behind him, can make himself distinguished.

¶ The Brotherhood of Consecrated Lives admits all who are worthy; and all who are excluded, exclude themselves. If your life is to be a genuine consecration, you must be free. Only the free man is truthful; only the heart that is free is pure.

¶ Instinct has a lucidity that surpasses wisdom.

¶ Very rightly the question comes in: If marriage is a lottery, why don't they arrest the minister?

❧ An ounce of performance is worth a pound of preachment.

❧ A normal impulse is a better guide than a fool sense of duty.

❧ To look upon the beauty of the world and realize the sorrow of mankind, and still prize and appreciate both the beauty and the sorrow, is to approximate the divine.

❧ We used to hear much about mere man, but man is now fast growing less mere.

❧ Advertising is the education of the public as to who you are, where you are, and what you have to offer in way of skill, talent or commodity. The only man who should not advertise is the man who has nothing to offer the world in way of commodity or service.

❧ We reach infinity through the love of one, and loving this one we are in love with all.

❧ The beggar is a robber who has lost his nerve—a bandit with a streak of yellow in his ego.

¶ Beware of chums—they only pool their weaknesses. He is strongest who stands alone. Be a friend to all—stand by all—speak well of all.

¶ The difference between bad and good people is this: The bad people have the bad on the outside, and the good in; while good people have the good outside, and the bad in.

¶ All is one, and the sacred is that which serves.

¶ The crime of orthodoxy is its lack of faith. It believes too little.

¶ Great organizers are men who are able to distinguish between initiative and "freshness." And frequently the difference is very slight.

¶ You ask me the purpose of life? So far I have been taken only partly into the counsels of Omnipotence—and only so far as I know will I pretend to answer.

¶ A religious dogma is a metaphor frozen stiff.

¶ The idea that you can become wise and "good" by the persistent perusal of a book—any book—is the monopoly of the ignorant: no matter how intelligent they may be.

¶ What the world needs is a religion that is not denatured.

¶ Easy rests the head that wears the crown of honest thought.

¶ When the whips of the Furies have lashed us sorely, Pride still serenely smiles and we congratulate ourselves on having stood the ordeal. This is happiness!

¶ To grow old and never know it is to achieve the greatest possible success in life, next to growing old and never having your friends suspect it.

¶ Men who have ideas and express them are yet at bay in the world.

¶ Several things I do not know. One is, why the man on bad terms with dental floss talks to you at close range and aims for your features.

¶ And with all your getting, get busy.

¶ We never ask God to forgive anybody except where we have n't.

⁕

¶ To live for others to the exclusion of self tends to the annihilation of both.

⁕

¶ What this world needs is more wealth, not less.

⁕

¶ The supernatural is only the natural not yet understood.

⁕

¶ Socrates, Jesus, Savonarola, Old John Brown, and none of Freedom's illustrious dead died in vain. They died that we might live; and as a single drop of aniline will tint an entire cask of water, so has the blood of martyrs tinted the Spirit of the Times and given us a peculiar and different "Zeitgeist" from that which we would otherwise have had.

⁕

¶ Marriage is love's demitasse.

⁕

¶ The only sure-enough businessman is the one who secures the business—the rest are clerks.

⁕

¶ No woman is a lady to her chauffeur.

132

¶A denial without an accusation is equal to a confession of guilt.

¶The things that should be left unsaid are often the things we like best to hear.

¶The most intolerant people in the world are those married ladies who cry "scab" at the woman who trespasses on their preserve without a union-card.

¶A true Roycrofter believes that only one person should get angry at a time. 17

¶Repeated failures probably prove that the world is on to your curves.

¶Little minds are interested in the extraordinary; great minds in the commonplace.

¶Be gentle and keep your voice low.

¶There is but one serious objection to Eden —the snake.

¶The guinea is a showy bird, but it takes a stork to deliver the goods.

¶A lawyer collected six hundred forty-one dollars for a client. The agreement was that the lawyer was to have ten per cent as a commission. How much did the client receive?

¶Taste is the final test — in other words, tell me what you like and I'll tell you what you are.

¶You are what you think, and to believe in a Hell for other people is literally to go to Hell yourself.

¶Recipe: Concentrate, Consecrate, Work.

¶Motto for a barber: Life is only a love-scrape.

¶Laugh with folks—not at them.

¶The prophet without honor is one who does not know how to advertise.

¶ Cheer up!—there is always room at the bottom.

¶ Manners make the man, but too much of them the fellow.

¶ When you accept a present, you have dissolved the pearl of independence in the vinegar of obligation.

¶ Keep up your nerve—a bull calf today may be at the head of the herd next year.

¶ When sinners entice thee, consent thou not —but take the name and address for future reference.

¶ If you can't be clever, don't be discouraged —you can still be fresh.

¶ I'll believe it when girls of twenty with money marry male paupers, turned sixty.

¶ The man who has no enemies isn't anybody and has never done anything.

¶ Don't make excuses—make good!

¶ Some women get old before they know it, but not many.

¶ We work not to acquire, but to become.

¶ Academic education is the act of memorizing things read in books, and things told by college professors who got their education mostly by memorizing things read in books and told by college professors.

¶ May Irwin writes that while a live husband may be a necessity, a dead one is a luxury.[18]

¶ Why not tabu the gabfest?

¶ Eat and drink just what you need; but don't be general manager of a swill-barrel.

¶ All good men suck eggs, but those who are wise hide the shells.

¶ Fences are only for those who can not fly.

¶ Life is just one damn thing after another.

¶ The alimentary canal is thirty-two feet long. You control only the first three inches of it. Control it well.

¶ The employee who is willing to steal for you will probably steal from you if he gets a chance.

¶ Pleasure-seekers never find theirs.

¶ Only wise men know how to play the fool.

¶ The world rewards cleverness before it does honesty. That is why I have n't got mine.

¶ If you do not agree with popular superstitions, you 'd better stand back to the wall.

¶ Beware of the doctor who talks about "cure," instead of looking for the cause. There is nothing to be gained by curing a symptom.

¶ If you have never made a fool of yourself, you are not in my class.

¶ The last word is this: Nothing matters, and no difference what happens the end is well. But wisdom consists in hustling just the same.

¶ A woman is known by the man she keeps.

¶ The ink of the wise is of more value than the blood of the martyrs.

—

¶ An Epigram: A vividly expressed truth that is so, or not, as the case may be.

—

¶ History: A collection of epitaphs.

—

¶ If you 've got a devil, put him to work.

—

¶ Your instincts are never wrong, but beware of psychic cramps. —

¶ Heaven is a habit, and so is Hell.

—

¶ An enemy is a counter-irritant. Get a few, or it 's you for fatty degeneration of the cerebrum. —

¶ There is no joy in life equal to the joy of putting salt on the tail of an idea.

—

¶ Happiness is a habit—cultivate it.

—

¶ Thought is conscious force—language is only a spigot. Most people need a plumber.

¶ Anger is the sweat of thought—verily, verily, a death-sweat!

⌐

¶ As long as a woman can pass for her daughter she is fairly satisfied.

⌐

¶ Truth is a useful idea.

⌐

¶ There are men who dare do anything, but who turn pale when Mrs. Grundy gets out her knitting and edges up.

⌐

¶ Bedbugs are all right—except when acting in their official capacity.

⌐

¶ It is the finest thing in the world to live—most people only exist.

⌐

¶ A woman over thirty who will tell her actual age will tell anything—watch her.

⌐

¶ When you are shocked, neither leave the room nor laugh—both are vulgar.

⌐

¶ Jesus loved fishermen — they have such hope.

¶ An imitator is a man who succeeds in being an imitation.

¶ Farmers are only half as stupid as most folks believe them to be, and Chicago people are only half as smart as they think they are.

¶ At what age does a woman cease to be Bessie and become Elizabeth? Altogether, now!

¶ Give me the man who, instead of always telling you what should be done, goes ahead and does it.

¶ Men are not equal in stupidity and foolishness: some have others skun a mile.

¶ Goethe once said, "He is happiest, king or peasant, who finds his happiness at home." And Goethe knew—because he never found it.

¶ Man's greatest blunder has been in trying to make peace with the skies instead of making peace with his neighbor.

¶ Boys will be boys and girls will be girls, but not forever.

¶ Opinion, Faith, Belief—so much dust that gathers on the abandoned machinery of thought.

¶ Grief is great raw stock for Art, but a bad thing to grab onto and keep.

¶ The new definition of a heathen is a man who has never played baseball.

¶ Doubt, unrest, fear and hatred reproduce their kind. To separate the unmated is a duty we owe the unborn.

¶ We legalize what we want to do, then we penalize what we don't want other people to do to us, and we call that justice.

¶ Love is the one Divine thing in the Universe. God has it in His special keeping.

¶ Man has not only "Seven Ages," but many more, and he must pass through this before the next arrives.[19]

¶ This religious farce is a hell of a play.

¶ Success : A constant sense of discontent, broken by brief periods of satisfaction on doing some specially good piece of work.

¶ An Unfortunate Female is a woman who can not live up to her indiscretions.

¶ Opportunity knocks once at every man's door, but if you, yourself, happen to be knocking when she calls, you'll never hear her.

¶ The modern sure-enough saint is the businessman who sticks to the one-price system and tells the truth.

¶ Faith in yourself and faith in humanity is faith in God.

¶ Debt is a rope to your foot, cockleburs in your hair, and a clothespin on your tongue.

¶ There is nothing breaks so many friendships as a difference of opinion as to what constitutes wit.

¶ Thirty-two is an attractive age. Many like it so well that they cling right there.

¶ When a man ceases to love a woman, her dress no longer seems to fit in the back, she bunches where she ought not to, and leaves unbunched the places she should bunch.

¶ Build your art horse-high, pig-tight and bull-strong.

¶ Sorrow is a job-lot of secondhand joy.

¶ Every human being is born beneath a signboard which reads, "To——! "

¶ Time is an illusion—to orators.

¶ No man will long be loyal to a woman who fails to laugh at his jokes.

¶ When you have failed at most everything, do not be discouraged—just prepare a lecture on "Success" and barnstorm the Chautauquas.

¶ If truth is not charming, bottle it.

¶ Beware of the actor who takes his fur overcoat seriously—or yours.

¶ An optimist is a man who when he falls in the soup thinks of himself as being in the swim.

¶ Civilization is largely a matter of buttoning and unbuttoning.

¶ To get into the best society nowadays, one has either to amuse people, feed people or shock people.

¶ The book of life begins with a man and a woman in a garden. It ends with Revelations.

¶ One thing, even if gasoline is not exactly the odor of roses, it does not breed flies.

¶ Did you ever hear of the woman who consulted a lawyer and explained that she wanted a divorce if she could n't get it, and if she could, she did n't want it?

¶ A woman who can not make her mistakes charming is only a female.

¶ Be patient with the fools: you may be one yourself pretty soon.

¶ A college degree, like a certificate of character, is a good thing for those who need it.

¶ He is best educated who is most useful.

¶ There is nothing new under the sun or a harem skirt.

¶ Never explain: your friends don't require it, and your enemies won't believe you anyway.

¶ Secrets are things we give to others to keep for us.

¶ Fit yourself for the best society in the world, and then keep out of it.

¶ Don't tell what you would do if you were some one else—just show what you can do yourself.

¶ Bloomingdale is not a place—not a locality. It is a condition of mind. [20]

¶ A lazy man is no more use than a dead one and takes up more room.

¶ Few women can keep a secret, even with salicylic acid. (Neither can men.)

¶ People who are happily married are those who do not scrap in public.

¶ Art is largely a matter of hair-cut.

¶ The cheerful loser is a winner.

¶ The graveyards are full of people the world could not do without.

¶ Following the Inner Light: Doing what you want to do in spite of Hell.

¶ People who do not spend their money until they get it are the only ones who are really on a solid footing.

¶ Those who can, do; those who can not, organize a class and show others how.

¶ You had better be an Is-Now than a Has-Wasser; and as for a Not-Yet-But-Soon, why he is always one.

¶ Man can not thrive apart from the land.

¶ The way to begin living the ideal life is to begin.

¶ Graft, grand or petty, is moral, financial and spiritual skidoo for any man who indulges in it.

¶ This will never be a civilized country until we spend more money for books than we do for chewing-gum.

¶ To use the word "Commercial" as an epithet is the mark of a Remittance-Man. The business that is not commercial has no excuse for being.

¶ I am not sure I should know a Blessing if I should meet it coming down the street —they dress that tarnashun queer, you know.

¶ No one who loves misunderstands.

¶ Just you please listen to my advice: Take nobody's.

¶ Everything done in hate has to be done over again.

¶ Complete success alienates a man from his fellows, but suffering makes kinsmen of us all.

¶ The trouble with many married people is that they are trying to get more out of marriage than there is in it.

¶ There are bigger magazines than "The Philistine," but I hope you understand that radium is worth more than coal. [21]

¶ Action will remove the doubt that theory can not solve.

¶ The object of education is that a man may benefit himself by serving others.

¶ When what you have done in the past looks large to you, you have n't done much today.

¶ If you would be healthy and happy, do not give the sawbuck absent treatment.

¶ Without animation man is naught.

¶ Be very careful how you go into the Best Society. I know a man who ventured in, once, and sank over his ears. We got him out, but he was never any good afterwards.

¶ A man loves himself and marries his ideal, and then blames his wife because she does not live up to all the virtues he can imagine.

¶ I recommend a religion that will unite men, not divide them.

¶ Bring me cheerful messages or none.

¶ There is a difference between joyous work and joyless toil—it is love that lightens labor.

¶ Requisites for an all-round education are: Ambition, Aspiration, Application, Respiration, Perspiration.

¶ A man possessing initiative is a creator.

⁋ Spare the rod and save the child.

⁋ Any man who looks to doctors and medicine to make him well and keep him well is headed for the monkey-house.

⁋ The men who act their thought, and think little of their act, are the ones who score.

⁋ Fear is with the faithless, and faith is with the fearless.

⁋ Give the pups time and they will get their eyes open.

⁋ Be small and keep your voice loud—there is plenty of precedent!

⁋ A cigarettist: One who is late every morning and fresh every evening.

⁋ The more I see of men, the better I like my horse.

⁋ Many men think they are psychic when they are only seasick.

⁋ Success is in the blood.

¶ To hold your job, you better close your gob.

¶ Success does not consist in showing how bad your competitor is.

¶ One machine can do the work of fifty ordinary men. No machine can do the work of one extraordinary man.

¶ Sublime thoughts and great deeds are the children of married minds. A man alone is only half a man—it takes a man and a woman to complete the circuit.

¶ An executive: A man who can make quick decisions and is sometimes right.

¶ One can play comedy; two are required for melodrama; but a tragedy demands three.

¶ Genius is fine, but if it comes to a showdown, gumption is better.

¶ Only that is fair and beautiful which neither threatens, bribes, evades, demands nor supplicates.

¶ Self-knowledge, self-respect, self-reliance are the truth that will bring you truth.

¶ Quit blaming other people for your troubles—if you were big enough you would n't have any.

¶ Recipe for having beautiful children: be a beautiful parent.

¶ The man who says, "Money is n't everything," probably is in arrears to his landlady.

¶ Recipe for educating your children: Educate yourself.

¶ Men engaged in useful work are not vicious.

¶ To own things is not the whole dam Edam.

¶ It pays to be good—I once tried it.

¶ In a world where death is, there is no time for hate.

¶ I believe that love should be free—which is not saying that I believe in free love.

¶ Sympathy is the sum of all the virtues.

¶ There are people who are in trouble; but their woe is nothing to that of those who expect trouble.

¶ Life is a search for those against whom we can charge up our little weaknesses.

¶ The star sneakerino in every school is a cigarette-smoker—there are no exceptions.

¶ It is not the finding of a thing, but the making something out of it after it is found, that is really of consequence.

¶ Supply a practical, worthy ideal, and your hoodlum spirit is gone—and gone forever.

¶ All the world loves a lover; but not while the love-making is going on.

¶ Produce great pumpkins—the pies follow.

¶ A sorry compromise beats a good lawsuit.

¶ When you see a tomcat with his whiskers full of feathers, do not say "Canary!"— he'll take offense!

¶ Falling in love is a matter of intermittent propinquity. The cure is—propinquity.

¶ Only a big man is able to wear a nickname and carry it off jauntily.

¶ Sympathy and sentiment in right proportion are all right and are needed, but both must be used as the warp and woof of the practical.

¶ One half of all lawyers are rogues. All lawyers admit it; and I give no offense to any one by making the statement, as every lawyer who reads this will instantly place himself, in imagination, on the side of the virtuous and run over in his mind the lawyers whom he knows are sure-enough rascals.

¶ Society does not punish those who sin, but those who sin and conceal not cleverly.

¶ The bribers are abroad. Beware, if you are a woman, of selling your soul to a marital mahout, for that badge of respectability, a marriage-certificate.

¶Only in the fury of excess does one catch glimpses of the immortal truths. Ah! the divine excess in great things—the excess that shot Mont Blanc towards the stars, the excess of life force that sent Byron flaming through Europe, the excess that flung Verlaine into the gutter! [22]

¶Success is a matter of the red corpuscle.

¶To button your collar behind means that you are making progress crab-fashion.

¶It is easy to sympathize with the proletariat when you have nothing to give but advice.

¶Whatsoever God has joined together, no man can put asunder.

¶To allow celibates to regulate a thing in which they do not believe is the crowning blunder of Sociology.

¶To be good is to be in harmony with oneself. Discord is to be forced to be in harmony with others.

❡ One of the compensations in sin is that it saves a man from becoming a Pharisee.

❡ The charm of reading is in the recognition of what we know.

❡ The only way you can get into the Kingdom of Heaven is to carry the Kingdom of Heaven in your own heart.

❡ People who profess to love their enemies are apt to hold averages good by hating their friends.

❡ Positive anything is better than negative nothing.

❡ I do not care what a man has been. I care what he has become.

❡ Blessed is that man who does not belliake.

❡ Your neighbor is the man who needs you.

❡ In ethics you can not better the Golden Rule.

❡ When two men of equal intelligence and sincerity quarrel, both are probably right.

⁋ He who lives but to enjoy, never enjoys anything.

⁋ The only sure-enough sinner is the man who congratulates himself that he is without sin.

⁋ Art shows you the thing you might have done if you had had a mind.

⁋ Sensuality and asceticism at the last are one.

⁋ To lose one's self-respect is the only calamity.

⁋ Blessed is that man (or woman) who does not snoop.

⁋ The Eleventh Commandment is: Thou shalt not rubber.

⁋ Roycroft Suggestion No. 79 — Only one get mad at a time. [23]

⁋ All things come too late for those who wait.

⁋ The only man who makes money following the races is the one who does so with a broom and shovel.

It is better to turn around than to turn turtle.

Enter without knocking: and remain on the same terms.

To hold the old customers get out after the new.

Spinsterhood is not a misfortune—it is an achievement.

The husbands of very beautiful women belong to the criminal classes.

Only the shallow know themselves.

Whisky is the Devil's right bower.

The old believe everything; the middle-aged suspect everything; the young know everything.

We live in an age when unnecessary things are our only necessities.

Oratory is the lullaby of the intellect.

❡ Experience is the name every one gives his mistakes.

❡ Children begin by loving their parents; as they grow older they judge them—sometimes they forgive them.

❡ Enthusiasm is the great hill-climber.

❡ Money breaks into society—and society breaks into the Ten Commandments.

❡ An idea that is not dangerous is unworthy of being called an idea at all.

❡ Too many people nowadays know the price of everything and the value of nothing.

❡ Indulge an automobile appetite with a push-cart income, and it is you for the ram-jams and stripes.

❡ Many good men are good from lack of opportunity or an overplus of caution.

❡ Irony is the cactus-plant that sprouts over the tomb of our dead illusions.

❡The ideal life is only man's normal life as we shall some day know.

❡Indefinite and indefinable longings, abnegation, horsehair robes, rope-girdles, resignation unresigned, crucified hopes, stifled desires, smothered aspirations, and green cheese are not virtue.

❡Purity consists in being satisfied.

❡An ounce of loyalty is worth a pound of cleverness.

❡All are needed by each, and each is necessary to all.

❡If you want something, you should pray for it as if you had no hope on Earth, and work for it as if you expected no help from Heaven.

❡Health is free—the right state of mind will fetch it. Be a Philistine! 24

❡Defeat is only for those who accept it.

❡Disgrace consists in mentally acknowledging disgrace.

¶ There are a good many people who do not like what I write. To these I can only say: Do not be discouraged—you may yet grow to it.

¶ When man had evolved to a point where he loved one woman with an absorbing love, the rosy light of dawn appeared in the East, the Dark Ages sank into oblivion, and civilization kicked off the covers and cooed in the cradle.

¶ Is he sincere? Probably not, if he is always asking this question about others.

¶ Experience, like a marriage-certificate, is not transferable.

¶ Be yourself and you'll be distinguished.

¶ Fear less—hope more; eat less—chew more; whine less—breathe more; hate less —love more, and all good things are yours.

¶ The only difference between a saint and a sinner is that every saint has a past and every sinner has a future.

¶ About the only person who can make both ends meet, no matter how hard the times, is the lady contortionist.

¶ Disuse is misuse.

¶ No one but an aviator has the right to look down on others.

¶ When we say we are undone, we mean only that we have weakened and run up the white flag.

¶ It costs more to live now than ever before, but isn't it worth it?

¶ Raise a row and you will lower yourself.

¶ Orthodoxy is spiritual constipation.

¶ If the party is getting five hundred or more a week, you pronounce it Vodeveal. If he gets less than that sum, it is simply vau-de-ville.

¶ Suffering is one-half selfishness and the rest mostly hallucination.

¶ Virtue has many preachers, but few martyrs.

¶ The Hammer and Tongs are all right, but do not misuse them.

¶ The Comic Sunday Supplement is the Louvre of the proletariat.

¶ Slough your limitations.

¶ Most women love love more than they love their lover.

¶ Only the souls that have suffered are well loved.

¶ The celibacy that requires a vow is a form of immorality.

¶ On the questions of marriage and divorce, the clergy are making their last clutch.

¶ All I know of the love of God is what I see reflected in the eyes of her I love.

¶ Take the josh and let the credit go!

¶ To consume and destroy love by using it is the deliberate lunacy of civilized man.

¶ Saintship is the exclusive possession of those who have either worn out or never had the capacity to sin.

¶ Self-preservation prompts men to move in the line of least resistance.

¶ Self-reliance is all right, but independence is out of the question. No man gets along in life without the co-operation and support of other men.

¶ Sewing-machines and knitting-machines have done more to emancipate women than all the preachers.

¶ Small men are apologetic and give excuses for being on the earth and reasons for staying here so long. Not so the Great Souls. Their actions are regal, their language oracular, their manners affirmative.

¶ Society needs men who can serve it; humanity wants help—the help of strong, sensible, unselfish men.

¶ Our first and last demand of Art is that it shall give us the artist's best. Art is the mintage of the soul. All the whim, foible and rank personality are blown away on the winds of time—the good remains.

¶ I admire classical music—the other kind I enjoy.

¶ Genius may have its limitations, but stupidity is not thus handicapped.

¶ Some folks have more temptations than others because they are always hunting for them.

¶ On man's journey through life he is confronted by two tragedies. One when he wants a thing he can not get; and the other when he gets the thing and finds he does not want it.

¶ Some people would like the honor of having won a fast race, but want to go around the course in a Sedan chair.

¶Marriage, to the priest, is a form of sin. His words sanctify it, so he says.

⚊

¶The indissoluble marriage comes in first with women as a chattel.

⚊

¶If anything in life is divine it is human nature. Trust it! ⚊

¶Beware of the consecration that does not consecrate. ⚊

¶Freedom implies responsibility—the slave has neither. ⚊

¶How futile the precaution when only his collar is buttoned behind!

⚊

¶The tactics of the inkfish are not covered by copyright. ⚊

¶The idea that you can become wise and "good" by the persistent perusal of a book— any book—is the monopoly of the ignorant: no matter how intelligent they may be.

⚊

¶ Death is n't a calamity for the individual who dies, but the fear of death is.

¶ I am an Episcopalian to this extent: I have always done the thing I did not plan to do, and that which I planned to do I have not done.

¶ To the pure all things are impure.

¶ Attraction to lovers is in inverse ratio to the square of the distance.

¶ No man is damned eternally as long as he tries.

¶ If a man can write a better book, preach a better sermon or make a better mouse-trap than his neighbor, though he build his house in the woods, the world will make a beaten path to his door.

¶ Something for nothing is always paid for.

¶ The only man who is in danger of losing his soul is the one who fails to use his sky-piece.

¶ O God! we thank Thee that Thou hast given us faults and thereby made us men.

¶ Let this be a world of friends!

❧ Sometimes I think all the Children of Israel must have been mismated, otherwise the making of the Ten Commandments were a superfluity.

❧ Only wise men know how to play the fool.

❧ Some have counted sex a mistake on the part of God; but the safer view is for us to conclude that whatever is, is good; some things are better than others, but all are good.

❧ A punster is to a humorist what a burro is to a horse.

❧ Only the souls that have suffered are well loved.

❧ Truth is the opinion that still survives.

❧ Many a man looking for sympathy needs really two swift kicks properly placed.

❧ Your relatives are people who neither know how to live nor when to die.

¶The Twelfth Commandment is this: Do not take yourself too damn serious.

¶One thing I never try to do, and that is, scratch the back of a professional porcupine in order to secure his good-will.

¶Dope, booze, stuff, swill and hate—and you will have it, all right!

¶Joyous are the busy, dissatisfied the idle.

¶The stomach that lasts is the one that rebels if misused. Now perhaps you see why it is that delicate people live the longest.

¶Most men when in Rome not only do as the Romans do, but see them, and go them one better.

¶It's only the fellow on the outside who can tell a snail how his shell looks.

¶No person utterly miserable ever did a great work.

¶What the world needs is a Greedless Christianity.

¶ The wise man contains in himself every quality of the foolish person, plus the attributes and characteristics of the wise one. His foolishness is held in check by discretion, and instead of energy being blown about by caprice, it is controlled by judgment.

¶ If you are defamed let time vindicate you. Silence is a thousand times better than explanation.

¶ The world is run by second-rate people. The best are speedily crucified, or else never heard of until long after they are dead.

¶ Give me solitude, sweet solitude : but in my solitude give me still one friend to whom I may murmur, "Solitude is sweet."

¶ The world will be redeemed; it is being redeemed. It is being redeemed not by those who shake the red rag of wordy warfare, who threaten and demand, but by its enterprisers, workers, inventors, toilers—the men and women who do the duty that lies nearest them.

¶ They will talk anyway!

¶ The tragedy of existence lies in interposing that newly discovered thing called intellect into the delicate affairs of life, instead of having faith in God, and moving serenely with the eternal tide.

¶ Lost—While busily engaged in knocking the firm, an opportunity to make a sale.

¶ There are two kinds of people in this world—those who are always getting ready to do something, and those who go ahead and do it.

¶ He who giveth to the poor lendeth to the devil.

¶ The view of a valley is not lost to the climber of heights overlooking the same, and the new point of vantage may add transcending beauties—beyond the sight of those below.

¶ When you get angry it is Righteous Indignation; when the other fellow gets angry it is an exhibition of Beastly Temper.

¶ The Butterfly Business is all right until the Frost comes.

¶ Old maids rush in where widows fear to tread.

¶ People will believe in you if you set them the example.

¶ All the scale Ali Baba picks up—and he usually gets his own—he refers to as Ali mony.[25]

¶ Only a real-estate man should be contented with his lot.

¶ I know a Scotchman who always opens the window of his office before looking out, so as not to wear out the glass.

¶ Life is just one improper number after another.

¶ In good society, all women should be married and all men single.

¶ If you can neither fly nor climb, don't be discouraged—perhaps you can kick.

¶ "What's a Rear Admiral, Papa?" "Oh, don't bother me—a Rear Admiral is a boy swimming with his head under water."

¶ All mud sticks, but no mud is immortal.

¶ Men and women never leave their own.

¶ The Medical Trust would certainly have pronounced Jesus Christ an "irregular."

¶ When you marry you either have an aeroplane or a sinker.

¶ Leastwise, college gives a patent pedagogic social shine.

¶ A widow who marries the second time does n't deserve to be one.

¶ You 'd better be a sinner than a cast-iron monkey or a plaster-of-Paris cat. God will forgive the sinner, but what He will do with the prig is a problem.

¶ The apparel of the woman oft proclaims the man.

¶ To Purist: The term "Unqualified Liar" refers to a man who has assumed the activities of the profession before he has passed his finals.

¶The difference between an ethical and a non-ethical doctor is this: The non-ethical doctor is willing to pay for his advertising, and the other wants his advertising to go in as a news item and he will pay nothing.

⌐

¶Don't aspire to be King of the Grouch-erinos—there are too many candidates now.

⌐

¶To love one's friends, to bathe in the sunshine of life, to preserve a right mental attitude—the receptive attitude, the attitude of gratitude—and to do one's work—these make the sum of an ideal life.

⌐

¶Why not start a Belliakers' Trust, and give special rates on Pond's Extract?

⌐

¶To make a man exempt is to take away from him just so much manhood.

⌐

¶Marriage a la mode either makes you weep or yawn. But marriage a la carte—bless my soul, Geraldine, pass the salad!

⌐

¶To mediocrity genius is unforgivable.

¶ The man at his work! There is nothing finer. I have seen men homely, uncouth and awkward when "dressed up" who were superb when at work.

¶ Through sin do men reach the light.

¶ A man's god is the highest concept of what he would like to be: his god is himself at his best, his devil himself at his worst.

¶ Small men are provincial, mediocre men are cosmopolitan; but great souls are Universal.

¶ The world laughs with the man who laughs; if you do not laugh, the world will laugh at you.

¶ The true solace for all private troubles is to lose yourself in your work.

¶ Every fault is forgiven the man of perfect candor.

¶ The term "crank" is an expression used by people who have wheels to designate people who are similarly equipped.

¶ Doctors, lawyers and preachers only know one way to make money, and that is to get yours. And, usually, they do not care how they get it.

¶ That man only is great who utilizes the blessings that God provides; and of these blessings no gift equals the gentle, trusting companionship of a good woman.

¶ At the top of the Greek Olympus there were fresh air and the stars; at the top of Christian Cathedrals there are only bad breaths and missing words.

¶ To send the hearer away stepping light, and his heart beating fast—this is oratory.

¶ Expose not thyself by four-footed manners.

¶ To stand by the open grave of one you have loved and feel the sky shut down over less worth in the world is the supreme test.

¶ The meek shall inherit the earth, but the hustler will have the estate before the legatee can probate the will.

¶ To pardon is the privilege only of the living.

¶ Brace with booze and bromide and you are on the slide for Tophet, sure as hell.

¶ To repeat an unkind truth is just as bad as to invent a lie.

¶ A dollar in the bank is worth two in the bucket.

¶ The only kind of power the Pope has, or ever had, is temporal power.

¶ Impossible things are simply those which so far have never been done.

¶ The lickspittle is always a tyrant when he gets the chance.

¶ Don't join the Grouch Trust, or it is you for Class B and the toboggan.

¶ The tariff should be increased on foreign princes.

¶ Live your life—do not sell it for a mess of peace potash.

¶The reason opinions are so diverse concerning every strong man is that most people fix their attention on some particular phase of his character—some mere external eccentricity possibly, that is of no value, one way or the other. The whole is what makes up the character—not these trivial parts.

¶Don't slam the door of your sympathies on any one—you can't afford it.

¶The refinements of civilization are quite as dangerous as the frank brutalities of savagery.

¶Churches, like department-stores, carry the wares that are asked for.

¶There are three sides to every question —where a divorce is involved.

¶It is absurd to try to prove things: even truth can be proved—sometimes.

¶That which teaches can not be wholly bad.

The refluxes of the heart are as sure and certain as the march of the planets. The desires of the heart are fixed stars—clouds may obscure, but wait and you shall see the light.

The rigors of climate and the unkindness of a scanty soil may be good things. They are good, very excellent, provided you do not get more than your constitution requires.

A wife who hangs her new dresses on the floor is worse than a mortgage on the house.

The slogan of the theologians: Cough!

Be at peace with yourself, and you will be at peace with the world.

The soldier and the priest have wrecked every land where they have had the power. Let's now give the businessman a chance to build things up.

Truth is that which serves us best in expressing our lives. A rotting log is truth to a bed of violets; while sand is truth to a cactus.

What people need and what they want may be very different.

Truth lies at the end of a circle.

The human face is the masterpiece of God.

He is a sinner who nails a man because he is another.

A man is a god in the crib.

The only way to keep your education is to give it away.

Nothing is so fatal to integrity as pretense.

Trouble arises largely from each man regarding himself as his brother's keeper, and ceasing to be his friend.

¶To trust your heaven to your future is to have no future worth having.

⁌

¶We are traveling to the beautiful City of the Ideal. We are aware that we shall never reach it—but the suburbs are very pleasant. ⁌

¶To try many things means Power; to finish a few means Immortality.

⁌

¶More lives are blasted by secrecy than frankness—aye, a thousand times.

⁌

¶Truth is an imaginary line dividing error into two parts. ⁌

¶To feel, to think, to know, to live, aye! to suffer, are not small things—I'm glad I'm here. ⁌

¶Experience is the germ of power.

⁌

¶Truth is in the air, and when your head gets up in the right stratum of atmosphere you breathe it in. ⁌

¶It is a fine thing to be yourself.

¶ The source of **Power** is in human emotion —in human desire. Men get what they work for, and in just the measure they work for it. The measure of success is the measure of desire.

¶ Remember the week-day to keep it holy.

¶ The strength of the hands of men is not proven by assertion—it is proven by use.

¶ The formula for hate: Keep your eye on each other's deficiencies.

¶ If it was woman who put man out of Paradise, it is still woman, and woman only, who can lead him back.

¶ The strong are always those who have stood by open graves, and heard the clods echo on dead hopes and treasures priceless.

¶ The success of an individual is usually damnation for his children.

¶ The kindergarten is the greatest scheme ever devised for the education—of parents.

¶ Beware of the education de luxe.

¶ Trouble tries us.

¶ Depend upon it, the best remedy for decay is an active interest in human affairs.

¶ The epithet you apply to another man probably fits yourself best.

¶ Piety is pretty fair, but not so good as performance.

¶ Troubles are not really troubles unless you quit work and incubate them—otherwise they are only incidental diversions.

¶ An organization of men is a machine for doing five minutes' work in an hour.

¶ The real problem of life is how to live rightly in the world, not how to get away from it.

¶ Sickness is a result, and so is health.

❡ The things we do when fear and hate are at the helm are usually wrong, and certainly do not mirror our better selves.

❡ No disappointment is quite so bitter as the disappointment that comes when you are disappointed with yourself.

❡ The thing you believe in will probably benefit you—faith is hygienic.

❡ Would you make better men—set them an example!

❡ The thought of the love of God can not be grasped in the slightest degree, even as a working hypothesis, by a man who does not know human love.

❡ Politicians are men who volunteer the task of governing us for a consideration.

❡ The hands that help are better far than the lips that pray.

❡ If we carry any possession from this world, it is the memory of a great love.

The teacher is one who makes two ideas grow where only one grew before.

The teacher is one who makes two ideas grow where only one grew before.

Noah was six hundred years old before he knew how to build the ark—don't lose your grip !

Telescopes are not used for the same purpose that magnifying-glasses are.

That expression, "sinking self," is only a figure of speech. At the last the true artist never sinks self: he is always supreme and towers above every subject, every object that he portrays.

Your quarrel with the world is but a quarrel with yourself. Get in line with the planets.

That fear in certain instances has deterred men from crime there is no doubt. But the error of religion as a police system lies in the fact that it makes superstition perpetual.

¶ No person utterly miserable ever did a great work.

¶ That men should dogmatize concerning things where the senses alone supply the evidence, is only another proof of man's limitations.

¶ The age of enlightenment will not be here until every church has evolved into a school-house, and every preacher is both a teacher and a pupil.

¶ It is a greater disgrace to be sick than to be in the penitentiary. If you are in the pen, it is a sign that you have broken some man-made statute, but if you are sick it is a sign you have broken some God-made law.

¶ That man only is great who utilizes the blessings that God provides ; and of these blessings no gift equals the gentle, trusting companionship of a good woman.

NOTES

1. Lobsters; An opprobrius idiomatic term of the day.
2. Pi; A printing term meaning disaster, chaos or mess.
3. Buffalo Jones; Born in Illinois about 1835. His given name was Charles but because of his rare ability to tame wild horses and mules and his efforts to preserve the buffalo from near extinction he switched to the more euphonious and poetic name of "Buffalo."
4. Tumbo; In the Swahili language, tumbo means protuberance of the abdomen, stomach or womb. Hence, Bwana Tumbo would suggest the tyrannical, notorious master demanding propagation in order to achieve the "masses" who fertilize the glory of the great!
5. Jacaseria; Jaca or jackfruit is an East Indian tree (closely related to bread-fruit) widely cultivated in tropics for its immense fruits which contain an edible

NOTES

but insipid pulp. "Seria"—of or relating to!

6. Chicago Tongue; In 1900 Hubbard wrote an article entitled "Chicago Tongue" in which he berated the "gossiper" who lent his ear to all plots, listened to and enjoyed all scandal, told much bad news and gloried in any man's downfall.

7. Garcia; Hubbard's classic essay dealing with initiative, entitled "A Message to Garcia."

8. Billy Sunday; William Ashley Sunday, (1863–1935) was first a baseball player but was converted to religious work about 1896 and became a well known evangelist. Hubbard called him the "World's great expert on the unknowable."

9. East Aurora; See "The Roycroft Shop: a History."

10. Chicago Tongue; See Note 6.

11. Yone Noguchi; A Japanese poet (1875–1947), who also wrote critical essays in English.

12. Bryan, William Jennings; The famous

American political leader and masterful orator.

13. The Philistine; Hubbard's little pocket magazine with the subtitle "A Periodical of Protest." This magazine was issued monthly from June, 1895, through July, 1915. It was in the March, 1899 issue that Hubbard's classic essay "A Message to Garcia" first appeared—without a title. This preachment has been translated into at least twenty foreign languages and over eighty million copies have been printed.

14. Setebos; A deity worshiped by the Patagonians. In Shakespeare's "The Tempest" he appears as the power worshiped by Sycorax (the witch).

15. A-Kneipping; "Kneipe," in German, means a beer house or tavern where German university students would gather for social drinking which usually ended in drinking bouts.

16. Cephalo-Genesis; Since the word "cephalo" pertains to the head, Hubbard probably coined this phrase to suggest the futility of "head butting."

NOTES

17. Roycrofter; See "The Roycroft Shop: a History."
18. May Irwin; A noted American comic actress (1862–1938).
19. "Seven Ages"; Shakespeare's "As You Like It," Act ii–Sc. 7, "All the world's a stage, . . . His acts being seven ages. At first the infant . . ."
20. Bloomingdale; A well known mental institution, Hubbard once addressed a heckling audience as "My friends from Bloomingdale."
21. Philistine; See Note 13.
22. Verlaine; Paul Verlaine (1844–96) was a French poet whose life was one of wretchedness. He wrote some noble religious poetry while in prison but through the degrading incidents of his later life, which was surrendered to drunkenness, poverty, and debauchery, he preserved his honesty and inverted naiveté.
23. Roycroft; See "The Roycroft Shop: a History."
24. Philistine; See Note 13.
25. Ali Baba; Hubbard wrote, "Ali Baba has

been my faithful friend and helper for near a score of years. To do good is his religion. At times when the way was dark with uncertainty and my plans seemed vanishing in mist, I have taken fresh courage when I thought of one who lives content with small means, talks gently, acts frankly, bears all cheerfully and does all bravely—for such is Ali Baba of East Aurora." See "The Roycroft Shops: a History."

INDEX

INDEX

INDEX

INDEX

INDEX

INDEX

INDEX

INDEX

INDEX

INDEX

INDEX

INDEX

SO HERE THEN ENDETH THIS MOST
WORTHY BOOK, *ONE THOUSAND AND
ONE EPIGRAMS*, THE SAME BEING
ORPHIC SAYINGS EVOLVED IN IDLE
MOMENTS BY ELBERT HUBBARD AND
GATHERED TOGETHER AND DONE
INTO A PRINTED VOLUME BY THE
ROYCROFTERS AT THEIR SHOP, AT
EAST AURORA, IN THE YEAR MCMXI.

The Roycroft Shop

A HISTORY

BY ELBERT HUBBARD

DONE INTO A BOOKLET BY THE ROYCROTERS AT
THEIR SHOP WHICH IS IN EAST AURORA, ERIE
COUNTY, NEW YORK, U. S. A., JULY, MCMVIII

THE editor of "The Cosmopolitan Magazine" has asked me to write an article for publication about myself and the work in which I am engaged.

I think I am honest enough to sink self, to stand outside my own personality, and answer the proposition ❧ Let me begin by telling what I am not, and thus reach the vital issue by elimination.

First. I am not popular in "Society," and those who champion my cause in my own town are plain, unpretentious people.

Second. I am not a popular writer, since my name has never been mentioned in the "Atlantic," "Scribner's," "Harper's," "The Century" or the "Ladies' Home Journal." But as a matter of truth, it may not be amiss for me to say that I have waited long hours in the entry way of each of the magazines just named, in days agone, and then been handed the frappe.

Third. I am not rich, as the world counts wealth.

Fourth. As an orator I am without the graces, and do scant justice to a double-breasted Prince Albert.

Fifth. The Roycroft Shop, to the welfare of which my life is dedicated, is not so large as to be conspicuous on account of size.

Sixth. Personally, I am no ten-thousand-dollar beauty: the glass of fashion and the mold of form are far from mine ❧ ❧

Then what have I done concerning which the public wishes to know? Simply this:

In one obscure country village I have had something

to do with stopping the mad desire on the part of the young people to get out of the country and flock to the cities. In this town and vicinity the tide has been turned from city to country. We have made one country village an attractive place for growing youth by supplying congenial employment, opportunity for education and healthful recreation, and an outlook into the world of art and beauty.

All boys and girls want to make things with their hands, and they want to make beautiful things, they want to "get along," and I've simply given them a chance to get along here, instead of seeking their fortunes in Buffalo, New York or Chicago. They have helped me and I have helped them; and through this mutual help we have made head, gained ground upon the whole. ¶ By myself I could have done nothing, and if I have succeeded, it is simply because I have had the aid and co-operation of cheerful, willing, loyal and loving helpers. Even now as I am writing this in my cabin in the woods, four miles from the village, they are down there at the Shop, quietly, patiently, cheerfully doing my work—which work is also theirs. No man liveth unto himself alone: our interests are all bound up together, and there is no such thing as a man going off by himself and corralling the good.

When I came to this town there was not a house in the place that had a lavatory with hot and cold water attachments. Those who bathed, swam in the creek in the summer or used the family washtub in the kitchen in winter. My good old partner, Ali Baba, has always prided himself on his personal cleanliness. He

2

is arrayed in rags, but underneath, his hide is clean, and better still, his heart is right. Yet when he first became a member of my household, he was obliged to take his Saturday-night tub out in the orchard from spring until autumn came, with withered leaves. He used to make quite an ado in the kitchen, heating the water in the wash-boiler. Six pails of cistern-water, a gourd of soft soap and a gunny sack for friction were required in the operation. Of course the Baba waited until after dark before performing his ablutions. But finally his plans were more or less disturbed by certain rising youth, who timed his habits and awaited his disrobing with o'er-ripe tomatoes. The bombardment, and the inability to pursue the enemy, turned the genial current of the Baba's life awry until I put a bathroom in my house, with a lock on the door. This bit of history I have mentioned for the dual purpose of shedding light on former bathing facilities in East Aurora, and more especially to show that once we had the hoodlum with us.

❡ Hoodlumism is born of idleness; it is useful energy gone to seed. In small towns hoodlumism is rife, and the hoodlums are usually the children of the best citizens. Hoodlumism is the first step in the direction of crime. The hoodlum is very often a good boy who does not know what to do; and so he does the wrong thing. He bombards with tomatoes a good man taking a bath, puts tick-tacks on windows, ties a tin can to the dog's tail, takes the burrs off your carriage-wheels, steals your chickens, annexes your horse-blankets and scares old ladies into fits by appearing at windows wrapped in a white sheet. To wear a mask, walk in and demand

3

the money in the family ginger-jar is the next and natural evolution.

To a great degree the Roycroft Shop has done away with hoodlumism in this village, and a stranger wearing a silk hat, or an artist with a white umbrella, is now quite safe upon our streets. Very naturally, the Oldest Inhabitant will deny what I have said about East Aurora—he will tell you that the order, cleanliness and beauty of the place have always existed. The change has come about so naturally, and so entirely without his assistance, that he knows nothing about it. Truth when first presented is always denied, but later there comes a stage when the man says, "I always believed it." And so the good old citizens are induced to say that these things have always been, or else they gently pooh-pooh them. However, the truth remains that I introduced the first heating-furnace into the town; bought the first lawn-mower; was among the first to use electricity for lights and natural gas for fuel; and so far, am the only one in town to use natural gas for power.

Until the starting of the Roycroft Shop there were no industries here, aside from the regulation country store, grocery, tavern, blacksmith-shop and sawmill —none of which enterprises attempted to supply more than local wants. There was Hamlin's stock-farm, devoted to raising trotting-horses, that gave employment to some of the boys; but for the girls there was nothing. They got married at the first chance; some became "hired girls," or if they had ambitions, fixed their hearts on the Buffalo Normal School, raised tur-

4

keys, picked berries, and turned every honest penny towards the desire to get an education so as to become teachers. Comparatively, this class was small in number. Most of the others simply followed that undefined desire to get away out of the dull, monotonous, gossiping village; and so, craving excitement, they went away to the cities and the cities swallowed them. A wise man has said that God made the country, man the city, and the devil the small towns.

The country supplies the cities its best and worst. We hear of the few who succeed, but of the many who are lost in the maelstrom we know nothing. Sometimes in country homes it is even forbidden to mention certain names. "She went to the city"—you are told, and there the history abruptly stops.

And so, to swing back to the place of beginning, I think the chief reason many good folks are interested in the Roycroft Shop is because here country boys and girls are given work at which they can not only earn their living, but get an education while doing it. Next to this is the natural curiosity to know how a large and successful business can be built up in a plain, humdrum village by simply using the talent and materials that are at hand, and so I am going to tell now how the Roycroft Shop came to start; a little about what it has done; what it is trying to do; and what it hopes to become ❧ And since modesty is only egotism turned wrong-side-out, I will make no special endeavor to conceal the fact that I have had something to do with the venture.

In London, from about Sixteen Hundred and Fifty to Sixteen Hundred and Ninety, Samuel and Thomas Roycroft printed and made very beautiful books. In choosing the name "Roycroft" for our shop we had these men in mind, but beyond this the word has a special significance, meaning King's Craft—King's craftsmen being a term used in the Guilds of the olden times for men who had achieved a high degree of skill—men who made things for the King. So a Roycrofter is a person who makes beautiful things, and makes them as well as he can. "The Roycrofters" is the legal name of our institution. It is a corporation, and the shares are distributed among the workers. No shares are held by any one but Roycrofters, and it is agreed that any worker who quits the Shop, shall sell his shares back to the concern. This co-operative plan, it has been found, begets a high degree of personal diligence, a loyalty to the institution, a sentiment of fraternity and a feeling of permanency among the workers that is very beneficial to all concerned. Each worker, even the most humble, calls it "Our Shop," and feels that he is an integral and necessary part of the Whole. Possibly there are a few who consider themselves more than necessary. Ali Baba, for instance, it is said, has referred to himself, at times, as the Whole Thing. And this is all right, too—I would never chide an excess of zeal: the pride of a worker in his worth and work is a thing to foster. It's the man who "does n't give a damn" who is really troublesome. The artistic big-head is not half so bad as apathy.

❧ ❧ ❧

IN the month of December, Eighteen Hundred and Ninety-four, I printed the first "Little Journeys" in booklet form, at the local printing-office, having

6

become discouraged in trying to find a publisher. But before offering the publications to the public, I decided to lay the matter again before G. P. Putnam's Sons, although they had declined the matter in manuscript form. Mr. George H. Putnam rather liked the matter and was induced to issue the periodical at a venture for one year. The scheme seemed to meet with success, the novel form of the publication being in its favor ✿ The subscription reached nearly a thousand in six months; the newspapers were kind and the success of the plan suggested printing a pamphlet modeled on similar lines, telling what we thought about things in general, and publishers and magazine editors in particular ✿ ✿

There was no intention at first of issuing more than one number of this pamphlet, but to get it through the mails at magazine rates we made up a little subscription list and asked that it be entered at the post-office at East Aurora as second-class matter. The postmaster adjusted his brass-rimmed spectacles, read the pamphlet, and decided that it surely was second-class matter ✿ ✿

We called it "The Philistine" because we were going after the "Chosen People" in literature. It was Leslie Stephen who said, "The term Philistine is a word used by prigs to designate people they do not like." When you call a man a bad name, you are that thing—not he. The Smug and Snugly Ensconced Denizens of Union Square called me a Philistine, and I said, "Yes, I am one, if a Philistine is something different from you."

¶ My helpers, the printers, were about to go away to

pastures new; they were in debt, the town was small, they could not make a living. So they offered me their outfit for a thousand dollars. I accepted the proposition.
¶ I decided to run "The Philistine" magazine for a year —to keep faith with the misguided and hopeful parties who had subscribed—and then quit. To fill in the time, we printed a book: we printed it like a William Morris book—printed it just as well as we could. It was cold in the old barn where we first set up "The Philistine," so I built a little building like an old English chapel right alongside of my house. There was a basement, and one room up-stairs. I wanted it to be comfortable and pretty, and so we furnished our little shop cozily. We had four girls and three boys working for us then. The shop was never locked, and the boys and girls used to come around evenings. It was really more pleasant than at home.

I brought over a shelf of books from my library. Then I brought the piano, because the youngsters wanted to dance ✧ ✧

The girls brought flowers and birds, and the boys put up curtains at the windows. We were having a lot o' fun, with new subscriptions coming in almost every day, and once in a while an order for a book.

The place got too small when we began to bind books, so we built a wing on one side; then a wing on the other side. To keep the three carpenters busy who had been building the wings, I set them to making furniture for the place. They made the furniture as good as they could—folks came along and bought it.

The boys picked up field stones and built a great, splendid

8

fireplace and chimney at one end of the shop. The work came out so well that I said: "Boys, here is a great scheme—these hardheads are splendid building material." So we advertised we would pay a dollar a load for niggerheads. The farmers began to haul stones; they hauled more stones, and at last they had hauled four thousand loads. We bought all the stone in the dollar limit, bulling the market on boulders.

Three stone buildings have been built, another is in progress, and our plans are made to build an art gallery of the same material—the stones that the builders rejected ✣ ✣

An artist blew in on the way to Nowhere, his baggage a tomato-can. He thought he would stop over for a day or two—he is with us yet, and three years have gone by since he came, and now we could not do without him. ¶ Then we have a few Remittance Men, sent to us from a distance, without return tickets. Some of these men were willing to do anything but work—they offered to run things, to preach, to advise, to make love to the girls ✣ ✣

We bought them tickets to Chicago and without violence conducted them to the Four o'Clock train.

We have boys who have been expelled from school, blind people, deaf people, old people, jailbirds and mental defectives, and have managed to set them all at useful work; but the Remittance Man of Good Family, who smokes cigarettes in bed, has proved too much for us—so we have given him the Four o'Clock without ruth.

We do not encourage people from a distance who want

9

work to come on—they are apt to expect too much. They look for Utopia, when work is work, here as elsewhere. There is just as much need for patience, gentleness, loyalty and love here as anywhere. Application, desire to do the right thing, a willingness to help, and a well-curbed tongue are as necessary in East Aurora as in Tuskegee.

We do our work as well as we can, live one day at a time, and try to be kind.

❧ ❧ ❧

THE village of East Aurora, Erie County, New York, the home of The Roycrofters, is eighteen miles southeast of the city of Buffalo. The place has a population of about two thousand people.

There is no wealth in the town and no poverty. In East Aurora there are six churches, with pastors' salaries varying from three hundred to one thousand dollars a year; and we have a most excellent school. The place is not especially picturesque or attractive, being simply a representative New York State village. Lake Erie is ten miles distant, and Cazenovia Creek winds its lazy way along by the village.

The land around East Aurora is poor, and so reduced in purse are the farmers that no insurance company will insure farm property in Erie County under any conditions unless the farmer has some business outside of agriculture—the experience of the underwriters being that when a man is poor enough, he is also dishonest; insure a farmer's barn in New York State and there is a strong probability that he will soon invest in kerosene.

¶ However, there is no real destitution, for a farmer

can always raise enough produce to feed his family, and in a wooded country he can get fuel, even if he has to lift it between the dawn and the day.

Most of the workers in the Roycroft Shop are children of farming folk, and it is needless to add that they are not college-bred, nor have they had the advantages of foreign travel. One of our best helpers, Uncle Billy Bushnell, has never been to Niagara Falls, and does not care to go. Uncle Billy says if you stay at home and do your work well enough, the world will come to you; which aphorism the old man backs up with another, probably derived from experience, to the effect that a man is a fool to chase after women, because if he does n't, the women will chase after him.

The wisdom of this hard-headed old son of the soil— who abandoned agriculture for art at seventy—is exemplified in the fact that during the year just past, over twenty-eight thousand pilgrims have visited the Roycroft Shop—representing every state and territory in the Union and every civilized country on the globe, even far-off Iceland, new Zealand and the Isle of Guam.

❡ Three hundred and ten people are on the pay-roll at the present writing. The principal work is printing, illuminating and binding books ✄ We also work at ornamental blacksmithing, cabinet work, painting pictures, clay-modeling and terra cotta. We issue two monthly publications, "The Philistine" magazine and "Little Journeys."

"The Philistine" has a circulation of a little over one hundred thousand copies a month, and we print sixty thousand copies of "Little Journeys" each issue. Most

11

of the "Journey" booklets are returned to us for binding, and nearly one-half of "The Philistine" magazines come back for the same purpose. The binding of these publications is simple work, done by the girls and boys we have educated in this line.

Quite as important as the printing and binding is the illuminating of initials and title-pages. This is a revival of a lost art, gone with so much of the artistic work done by the monks of the olden time ஃ Yet there is a demand for such work, and so far as I know, we are the first concern in America to take up the hand-illumination of books as a business. Of course we have had to train our helpers, and from very crude attempts at decoration we have attained to a point where the British Museum and the "Bibliotheke" at the Hague have deigned to order and pay good golden guineas for specimens of our handicraft. Very naturally we want to do the best work possible, and so self-interest prompts us to be on the lookout for budding genius. The Roycroft is a quest for talent.

ஃ ஃ ஃ

THERE are no skilled people in the Roycroft Shop, except those who have become skilled since they came here, with a very few exceptions. Among these is Mr. Louis H. Kinder, master bookbinder, who spent seven years' apprenticeship in Leipsic learning his trade ஃ Competent bibliophiles assure me that Mr. Kinder's work is not surpassed by that of any other bookbinder in America. I have specimens of the work done by Riviere, Zahn, Cobden-Sanderson, Zahnsdorf, "The Guild of Women Binders" of London and the

"Club Bindery" of New York; and we surely are not ashamed to show Mr. Kinder's work in the same case with these. But excellent and beautiful as Mr. Kinder's books are, his best work is in the encouragement and inspiration he has given to others.

Skilled artisans are usually so jealous of their craft that they refuse to teach others—not so Mr. Kinder ⚓ Through his patient tutorship there are now five helpers in our Shop who can fetch along a full levant book nearly to the finish ⚓ And besides that, there are forty others who can do certain parts well, and gradually are becoming skillful. It takes time to make a bookbinder: to bind a book beautifully, stoutly and well, and to hand-tool it is just as much of an art as to paint a beautiful picture.

In printing, our earlier attempts at "register" and "making ready" were often rather faulty, but with the aid of my faithful friends, we are doing work which I think ranks with the best. In the composition I have been especially helped by Charles Rosen, who set the type for our first book. This man has done for me the things I would have liked to do myself, but unfortunately I have only two hands and there are, so far, only twenty-four hours in a day. Happy is that man who has loyal, loving friends who are an extension of himself! ¶ There is a market for the best, and the surest way, we think, to get away from competition, is to do your work a little better than the other fellow ⚓ The old tendency to make things cheaper, instead of better, in the book line is a fallacy, as shown in the fact that within ten years there have been a dozen failures of

13

big publishing houses in the United States. The liabilities of these bankrupt concerns footed the fine total of fourteen million dollars. The man who made more books and cheaper books than any one concern ever made, had the felicity to fail very shortly, with liabilities of something over a million dollars. He overdid the thing in matter of cheapness—mistook his market. Our motto is, "Not How Cheap, But How Good."

This is the richest country the world has ever known, far richer per capita than England—lending money to Europe. Once Americans were all shoddy—pioneers have to be, I'm told—but now only a part of us are shoddy. As men and women increase in culture and refinement, they want fewer things, and they want better things. The cheap article, I will admit, ministers to a certain grade of intellect; but if the man grows, there will come a time when, instead of a great many cheap and shoddy things, he will want a few good things ❧ He will want things that symbol solidity, truth, genuineness and beauty.

The Roycrofters have many opportunities for improvement, not the least of which is the seeing, hearing and meeting distinguished people. We have a public dining-room, and not a day passes but men and women of note sit at meat with us. At the evening meal, if our visitors are so inclined, and are of the right fibre, I ask them to talk. And if there is no one else to speak, I sometimes read a little from William Morris, Shakespeare, Walt Whitman or Ruskin. David Bispham has sung for us. Maude Adams and Minnie Maddern Fiske have also favored us with a taste of their quality. Judge Lindsey,

14

Alfred Henry Lewis, Richard Le Gallienne, Robert Barr, have visited us, but to give a list of all the eminent men and women who have spoken, sung or played for us would lay me liable for infringement in printing "Who's Who." However, let me name one typical incident. The Boston Ideal Opera Company was playing in Buffalo, and Mr. Henry Clay Barnabee and half a dozen of his players took a run out to East Aurora. They were shown through the Shop by one of the girls whose work it is to receive visitors. A young woman of the company sat down at one of the pianos and played. I chanced to be near and asked Mr. Barnabee if he would not sing, and graciously he answered, "Fra Elbertus, I'll do anything that you say." I gave the signal that all the workers should quit their tasks and meet at the chapel. In five minutes we had an audience of three hundred—men in blouses and overalls, girls in big aprons—a very jolly, kindly, receptive company. ¶ Mr. Barnabee was at his best—I never saw him so funny. He sang, danced, recited, and told stories for forty minutes ❧ The Roycrofters were, of course, delighted. ¶ One girl whispered to me as she went out, "I wonder what great sorrow is gnawing at Barnabee's heart, that he is so wondrous gay!" Need I say that the girl who made the remark just quoted had drunk of life's cup to the very lees? We have a few such with us— and several of them are among our most loyal helpers.

❧ ❧ ❧

ONE fortuitous event that has worked to our decided advantage was "A Message to Garcia."
This article, not much more than a paragraph, cover-

ing only fifteen hundred words, was written one evening after supper, in a single hour. It was the Twenty-second of February, Eighteen Hundred and Ninety-nine, Washington's Birthday, and we were just going to press with the March "Philistine." The thing leaped hot from my heart, written after a rather trying day, when I had been endeavoring to train some rather delinquent helpers in the way they should go.

The immediate suggestion, though, came from a little argument over the teacups when my son Bert suggested that Rowan was the real hero of the Cuban war. Rowan had gone alone and done the thing—carried the message to Garcia.

It came to me with a flash! yes, the boy is right, the hero is the man who does the thing—does his work—carries the message.

I got up from the table, and wrote "A Message to Garcia."

I thought so little of it that we ran it in without a heading. The edition went out, and soon orders began to come for extra March "Philistines," a dozen, fifty, a hundred; and when the American News Company ordered a thousand I asked one of my helpers which article it was that had stirred things up.

"It's that stuff about Garcia," he said.

The next day a telegram came from George H. Daniels, of the New York Central Railroad, thus, "Give price on one hundred thousand Rowan article in pamphlet form—Empire State Express advertisement on back—also state how soon can ship."

I replied giving price and stated we could supply the

pamphlets in two years. Our facilities were small and a hundred thousand pamphlets looked like an awful undertaking.

The result was that I gave Mr. Daniels permission to reprint the article in his own way. He issued it in booklet form in editions of one hundred thousand each. Five editions were sent out, and then he got out an edition of half a million. Two or three of these half million lots have been sent out by Mr. Daniels, and in addition the article has been reprinted in over two hundred magazines and newspapers ❧ It has been translated into eleven languages, and been given a total circulation of over twenty-two million copies. It has attained, I believe, a larger circulation in the same length of time than any written article has ever before reached.

Of course, we cannot tell just how much good "A Message to Garcia" has done the Shop, but it probably doubled the circulation of both "Little Journeys" and "The Philistine." I do not consider it, by any means, my best piece of writing; but it was opportune—the time was ripe. Truth demands a certain expression, and too much had been said on the other side about the down-trodden, honest man looking for work and not being able to find it. The article in question states the other side. Men are needed, loyal, honest men who will do their work—"the world cries out for him—the man who can carry a message to Garcia."

The man who sent the message and the man who received it are dead. The man who carried it is still carrying other messages. The combination of theme, condition of the country, and method of circulation were so favorable that their conjunction will probably never occur again. Other men will write better articles, but they may go a-begging for lack of a Daniels to bring them to judgment.

❧ ❧ ❧

CONCERNING my own personal history, I'll not tarry long to tell. It has been too much like the career of many another born in the semi-pioneer times of the Middle West to attract much attention, unless one should go into the psychology of the thing with intent to show the evolution of a soul. But that will require a book—and some day I'll write it after the manner of St. Augustine or Jean Jacques.

But just now I'll only say that I was born in Illinois, June Nineteenth, Eighteen Hundred and Fifty-six. My father was a country doctor, whose income never exceeded five hundred dollars a year. I left school at fifteen, with a fair hold on the three R's, and beyond this my education in "manual training" had been good ❧ I knew all the forest trees, all wild animals thereabout, every kind of fish, frog, fowl or bird that swam, ran or flew. I knew every kind of grain or vegetable, and its comparative value. I knew the different breeds of cattle, horses, sheep and swine.

I could teach wild cows to stand while being milked, break horses to saddle or harness; could sow, plow and reap; knew the mysteries of apple butter, pumpkin pie, pickled beef, smoked side-meat, and could make lye at a leach and formulate soft soap. ¶ That is to say, I was a bright, strong, active country boy who had been brought up to help his father and mother get a living

18

for a large family. ¶ I was not so densely ignorant—
don't feel sorry for country boys: God is often on
their side ⚜ ⚜

At fifteen I worked on a farm and did a man's work
for a boy's pay. I did not like it and told the man so.
He replied, "You know what you can do."
And I replied, "Yes." I went westward like the course
of empire and became a cowboy; tired of this and went
to Chicago; worked in a printing-office; peddled soap
from house to house; shoved lumber on the docks;
read all the books I could find; wrote letters back to
country newspapers and became a reporter; next got
a job as traveling salesman; taught in a district school;
read Emerson, Carlyle and Macaulay; worked in a soap
factory; read Shakespeare and committed most of
"Hamlet" to memory with an eye on the stage; became
manager of the soap factory, then partner; evolved an
Idea for the concern and put it on the track of making
millions—knew it was going to make millions—did
not want them; sold out my interest for seventy-five
thousand dollars and went to Harvard College;
tramped through Europe; wrote for sundry newspapers; penned two books (could n't find a publisher);
taught night-school in Buffalo; tramped through
Europe some more and met William Morris (caught
it); came back to East Aurora and started "Chautauqua Circles"; studied Greek and Latin with a
local clergyman; raised trotting-horses; wrote "Little
Journeys to the Homes of Good Men and Great." ¶ So
that is how I got my education, such as it is. I am a
graduate of the University of Hard Knocks, and I 've

19

taken several postgraduate courses. I have worked at five different trades enough to be familiar with the tools. In Eighteen Hundred and Ninety-nine, Tufts College bestowed on me the degree of Master of Arts; but since I did not earn the degree, it really does not count ✌ ✌

I have never been sick a day, never lost a meal through disinclination to eat, never consulted a doctor, never used tobacco or intoxicants. My work has never been regulated by the eight-hour clause. ¶ Horses have been my only extravagance, and I ride horseback daily now: a horse that I broke myself, that has never been saddled by another, and that has never been harnessed.

My best friends have been workingmen, homely women and children. My father and mother are members of my household, and they work in the Shop when they are so inclined. My mother's business now is mostly to care for the flowers, and my father we call "Physician to the Roycrofters," as he gives free advice and attendance to all who desire his services. Needless to say, his medicine is mostly a matter of the mind. Unfortunately for him, we do not enjoy poor health, so there is very seldom any one sick to be cured. Fresh air is free, and outdoor exercise is not discouraged.

✌ ✌ ✌

THE Roycroft Shop and belongings represent an investment of about three hundred thousand dollars. We have no liabilities, making it a strict business policy to sign no notes, or other instruments of debt that may in the future prove inopportune and tend to disturb digestion. Fortune has favored us.

First, the country has grown tired of soft platitude, silly truism and undisputed things said in such a solemn way.So when "The Philistine" stepped into the ring and voiced in no uncertain tones what its editor thought, thinking men and women stopped and listened. Editors of magazines refused my manuscript because they said it was too plain, too blunt, sometimes indelicate—it would give offense, subscribers would cancel, et cetera. To get my thoughts published I had to publish them myself; and people bought for the very reason for which the editor said they would cancel. The readers wanted brevity and plain statement—the editors said they did n't ❧ ❧

The editors were wrong. They failed to properly diagnose a demand. I saw the demand and supplied it—for a consideration.

Next I believed the American public. A portion of it at least, wanted a few good and beautiful books instead of a great many cheap books. The truth came to me in the early nineties, when John B. Alden and half a dozen other publishers of cheap books went to the wall. I read the R. G. Dun & Company bulletin and I said, "The publishers have mistaken their public—we want better books, not cheaper." In Eighteen Hundred and Ninety-two, I met William Morris, and after that I was sure I was right.

Again I had guaged the public correctly—the publishers were wrong, as wrong as the editors ❧ There was a market for the best, and the problem was to supply it. At first I bound my books in paper covers and simple boards. Men wrote to me wanting fine bindings

21

—I said, there is a market in America for the best ❧ Cheap boards, covered with cloth, stamped by machinery in gaudy tinsel and gilt, are not enough ❧ I found that the bookbinders were all dead. I found five hundred people in a book factory in Chicago binding books, but not a bookbinder among them. They simply fed the books into hoppers and shot them out of chutes, and said they were bound. At last I discovered my Leipsic bookbinder, Louis Kinder, a silent man, with princely pride, who is sure that nobody but booklovers will go to heaven. He just wanted a bench and a chance to work—I supplied these, and here he is, doing the things I would like to do—doing them for me.

Next the public wanted to know about this thing— "What are you folks doing out there in that buckwheat town?" Since my twentieth year I have had one eye on the histrionic stage. I could talk in public a bit, had made political speeches, given entertainments in cross-road schoolhouses, made temperance harangues, was always called upon to introduce the speaker of the evening, and several times had given readings from my own amusing works for the modest stipend of ten dollars and keep. I would have taken the lecture platform had it not been nailed down.

In Eighteen Hundred and Ninety-eight, my friend Major Pond wanted to book me on a partnership deal at the Waldorf-Astoria. I did n't want to speak there —I had been saying unkind things in "The Philistine" about the Waldorf-Astoria folks. But the Major went ahead and made arrangements ❧ I expected to be mobbed ❧ ❧

22

But Mr. Boldt, the manager of the hotel, had placed a suite of rooms at my disposal without money and without price. He treated me most cordially; never referred to the outrageous things I had said about his tavern; assured me that he enjoyed my writings, and told me of the pleasure he had in welcoming me.

Thus did he heap hot cinders upon my occiput.

The Astor gallery seats eight hundred people. Major Pond had packed in nine hundred at one dollar each —three hundred were turned away. After the lecture the Major awaited me in the anteroom, fell on my neck and rained Pond's Extract down my back, crying, "Oh! Oh! Oh! ❧ Why did n't we charge them two dollars apiece!"

The next move was to make a tour of the principal cities under Major Pond's management. Neither one of us lost money—the Major surely did not.

Last season I gave eighty-one lectures, with a net profit to myself of a little over ten thousand dollars. I spoke at Tremont Temple, in Boston, to twenty-two hundred people; at Carnegie Hall, New York; at Central Music Hall, Chicago, I spoke to all the house would hold; at Chautauqua, my audience was five thousand people. It will be noted by the Discerning that my lectures have been of double importance, in that they have given an income and at the same time advertised the Roycroft Wares. ¶ The success of the Roycroft Shop has not been brought about by any one scheme or plan. The business is really a combination of several ideas, any one of which would make a paying enterprise in itself. So it stands about thus:

23

First. The printing and publication of two magazines. Second. The printing of books (it being well known that some of the largest publishers in America—Scribner and Appleton, for instance—have no printing plants, but have the work done for them). Third. The publication of books. Fourth. The artistic binding of books. Fifth. Authorship ❧ Since I began printing my own manuscript, there is quite an eager demand for my writing, so I do a little of Class B for various publishers and editors. Sixth. The Lecture Lyceum. Seventh. Blacksmithing, carpenter work, terra cotta and weaving. These industries have sprung up under the Roycroft care as a necessity ❧ Men and women, many of them seventy years young or so, in the village, came to us and wanted work, and we simply gave them opportunity to do the things they could do best ❧ We have found a market for all our wares, so no line of work has ever been a bill of expense.

I want no better clothing, no better food, no more comforts and conveniences than my helpers and fellow-workers have. I would be ashamed to monopolize a luxury—to take a beautiful work of art, say a painting or a marble statue, and keep it for my own pleasure and for the select few I might invite to see my beautiful things. Art is for all—beauty is for all. Harmony in all of its manifold forms should be like a sunset—free to all who can drink it in. The Roycroft Shop is for the Roycrofters, and each is limited only by his capacity to absorb.

❧ ❧ ❧

ART is the expression of man's joy in his work, and all the joy and love that you can weave into a fabric comes out again and belongs to the individual who has the soul to appreciate it ❧ Art is beauty, and beauty is a gratification, a peace and a solace to every normal man and woman. Beautiful sounds, beautiful colors, beautiful proportions, beautiful thoughts— how our souls hunger for them! Matter is only mind in an opaque condition; and all beauty is but a symbol of spirit ❧ ❧

You cannot get joy from feeding things all day into a machine. You must let the man work with hand and brain, and then out of the joy of this marriage of hand and brain, beauty will be born. It tells of a desire for harmony, peace, beauty, wholeness—holiness.

Art is the expression of man's joy in his work.

When you read a beautiful poem that makes your heart throb with gladness and gratitude, you are simply partaking of the emotion that the author felt when he wrote it. To possess a piece of work that the workman made in joyous animation is a source of joy to the possessor ❧ ❧

And this love of the work done by the marriage of hand and brain can never quite go out of fashion—for we are men and women, and our hopes and aims and final destiny are at last one. Where one enjoys, all enjoy; where one suffers, all suffer.

Say what you will of the coldness and selfishness of men, at the last we long for companionship and the fellowship of our kind. We are lost children, and when alone and the darkness gathers, we long for the close relationship of the brothers and sisters we knew in our childhood, and cry for the gentle arms that once rocked us to sleep. Men are homesick amid this sad, mad rush for wealth and place and power ✿ The calm of the country invites, and we would fain do with less things, and go back to simplicity, and rest our tired heads in the lap of Mother Nature.

Life is expression. Life is a movement outward, an unfolding, a development. To be tied down, pinned to a task that is repugnant, and to have the shrill voice of Necessity whistling eternally in your ears, "Do this or starve," is to starve; for it starves the heart, the soul, and all the higher aspirations of your being pine away and die.

At the Roycroft Shop the workers are getting an education by doing things. Work should be the spontaneous expression of a man's best impulses. We grow only through exercise, and every faculty that is exercised, becomes strong, and those not used atrophy and die. Thus how necessary it is that we should exercise our highest and best! ✿ To develop the brain we have to exercise the body. Every muscle, every organ, has its corresponding convolution in the brain. To develop the mind, we must use the body. Manual training is essentially moral training; and physical work is at its best mental, moral and spiritual—and these are truths so great and yet so simple that until yesterday many wise men did not recognize them.

At the Roycroft Shop we are reaching out for an all-round development through work and right living ✿ And we have found it a good expedient—a wise business policy. Sweat-shop methods can never succeed in producing beautiful things. And so the management of the Roycroft Shop surrounds the workers with ❧ beauty, allows many liberties, encourages cheerfulness and tries to promote kind thoughts, simply because it has been found that these things are transmuted into good, and come out again at the finger-tips of the workers in beautiful results. So we have pictures, statuary, flowers, ferns, palms, birds, and a piano in every room. We have the best sanitary appliances that money can buy; we have bathrooms, shower-baths, library, rest-rooms. Every week we have concerts, dances, lectures.

Beside being a workshop the Roycroft is a School. We are following out a dozen distinct lines of study, and every worker in the place is enrolled as a member of one or more classes ❧ There are no fees to pupils, but each pupil purchases his own books—the care of his books and belongings being considered a part of one's education. All the teachers are workers in the Shop, and are volunteers, teaching without pay, beyond what each receives for his regular labor.

The idea of teaching we have found is a great benefit —to the teacher ❧ The teacher gets most out of the lessons. Once a week there is a faculty meeting, when each teacher gives in a verbal report of his stewardship. It is responsibility that develops one, and to know that your pupils expect you to know is a great incentive to study. Then teaching demands that you shall give— give yourself—and he who gives most receives most. We deepen our impressions by recounting them, and he who teaches others teaches himself. I am never quite so proud as when some one addresses me as "teacher." We make a special feature, among our workers, of music. Our Musical Director is instructing over one hundred pupils of all ages, from three to seventy-three. We have a brass band, an orchestra, a choral society, a guitar and mandolin club, and a "Little German Band" that supplies the agrarians much glee.

We try to find out what each person can do best, what he wants to do, and then we encourage him to put his best into it—also to do something else besides his specialty, finding rest in change.

The thing that pays should be the expedient thing, and the expedient thing should be the proper and right thing. That which began with us as a matter of expediency is often referred to as a "philanthropy." I do not like the word, and wish to state here that the Roycroft is in no sense a charity—I do not believe in giving any man something for nothing. You give a man a dollar and the man will think less of you because he thinks less of himself; but if you give him a chance to earn a dollar, he will think more of himself and more of you. The only way to help people is to give them a chance to help themselves. So the Roycroft Idea is one of reciprocity—you help me and I'll help you. We will not be here forever, anyway: soon Death, the kind old Nurse, will come and rock us all to sleep, and we had better help one another while we may: we are going the same way—let's go hand in hand.

So here then endeth the Booklet entitled, THE ROYCROFT SHOP: A HISTORY, as written by Elbert Hubbard and done into print by THE ROYCROFTERS, at their shop which is in East Aurora, Erie County, New York, U. S. A., July, MCMVIII

The Greatest Mistake You Can Make in Life is to be Continually Fearing You Will Make One

ELBERT HUBBARD